"Terri Apple is a voice-over class act. Everyone who envies her rapid rise from retail clerk to voice-over star thinks it's all about her voice. Well, forget it. It isn't that simple. Without the combination of instinct and training that allows Terri to bring her "real self" to the work, that unique Terri Apple vocal sound would be meaningless. There are plenty of interesting voices out there, but where they fail is in trying to exclusively pin their hopes on the voice. Terri is a big hit with the ad community because she not only makes the text her own, but brings to every read the kind of truth that can only come by listening, answering and being in the moment. This unique story of how it happened for her and how it can happen for you could just be that special star someone can hitch a voice-over career onto, and make it soar—as she did."

—*DICK ORKIN, Owner, Radio Ranch,*
Writer, Producer, Director, V/O Actor

Making Money in Voice-overs

Winning Strategies to a Successful Career in TV, Commercials, Radio and Animation

by Terri Apple

ifilm publishing

MAKING MONEY IN VOICE-OVERS
Winning Strategies to a Successful Career
in TV, Commercials, Radio and Animation
Copyright © 1999 by Terri Apple

LONE EAGLE PUBLISHING COMPANY™
1024 N. Orange Drive
Hollywood, CA 90038
Phone 323.308.3400 or 800.815.0503
A division of IFILM® Corp., www.ifilm.com

Printed in the United States of America

Cover design by Lindsay Albert
Book design by Carla Green

Library of Congress Cataloging-in-Publication Data

Apple, Terri. 1964-
    Making money in voice-overs : winning strategies for a successful career in tv, radio, commercials and animation / by Terri Apple.
        p.   cm.
    ISBN 1-58065-011-2
    1. Television announcing—Vocational guidance. 2. Radio announcing—Vocational guidance. 3. Voice-overs. 4. Television advertising—Vocational guidance. 5. Radio advertising—Vocational guidance. I. Title.
    PN1992.8.A6 A66 1999
    791.4'023—dc21
                                                    98-45809
                                                    CIP

Books may be purchased in bulk at special discounts for promotional or educational purposes. Special editions can be created to specifications. Inquiries for sales and distribution, textbook adoption, foreign language translation, editorial, and rights and permissions inquiries should be addressed to: Jeff Black, IFILM Publishing, 1024 N. Orange Drive, Hollywood, CA 90038 or send e-mail to: info@ifilm.com

Distributed to the trade by National Book Network, 800-462-6420

IFILM® is a registered trademark.
Lone Eagle Publishing Company™ is a registered trademark.

CONTENTS

•••

• • •
FOREWORD
• • •

Hi, this is Gary Owens, and I want to welcome you! Thanks for buying such a very special book and for making such a special career choice . . . one in which I've made quite a career out of. I've been very lucky. It's quite a wonderful business, as you know—the voice-over field!

Terri Apple's voice-over book is a must for anyone trying to break into the business. I've done voice-overs for many years now, but Terri's book helps anyone at any level, from beginner to working professional. The insider tips and copy samples for practicing are immeasurably valuable. It's really great!

Good luck in your career.

—Gary Owens

• • •
INTRODUCTION
• • •

Welcome to the world of voice-overs—a very lucrative and reward-ing career choice. Many professionals in other fields have turned their part-time dabbling in voice-overs into full-time careers. (A friend of mine recently gave up his medical practice because he made more money, and spent less time doing voice-overs!)

People tell me, "I want to break into voice-overs." Well, this is your chance. Put one foot in front of the other, take a deep breath and . . . say the alphabet out loud. No, I'm serious. How's your diction? Your rhythm? Your range? Your resonance? Your accent? Your vocal level? Your inflection? Confused by the terms? Learning to do voice-overs is not always as easy as it seems. But if you suc-ceed, you will have made a great career choice than has been a secret in the "industry" for years. Anyone can succeed—men, women, and children. Age is no barrier, nor is appearance.

In the Beginning

From the time I was fifteen, I had the very deep, raspy, different voice that has become my trademark today. Friends told me that they thought I should do voice-overs. "Great!" I said, "What are they?" A friend's father who worked at an ad agency as a writer clued me in: The voices selling products on television and radio commercials were actually actors and actresses working in a field I'd never heard of before. Oftentimes the voices belonged to fa-mous celebrities, but more often than not, they belonged to ordi-nary actors and actresses.

I was hooked! This sounded like the perfect way for a full-time high school student to make some extra money. Who knew it would turn into a profitable career for me? I began the ground-work of making phone calls, finding agents who represented voice-over artists, finding out about a demo tape, making the tape, meeting the casting houses—in short, everything I needed to do from my end to get started.

I had a limited acting background. I'd been in some plays and done a little modeling. I listened to the radio and television to hear how the actors sounded. Selling the product always intrigued me. I loved acting and knew that this was just another way to act. I started to read the magazine ads into a tape recorder in several different ways and listened to the playback. I tried all different types of copy that I took from TV and radio. Eventually, I put together a homemade version on tape using my home equipment and started scouting for an agent. Since there were only two in my home town, this wasn't too difficult an objective. The first agent listened to my tape and kindly replied, "Have you thought about being a secretary?" This was my entry into voice-overs! It taught me to overcome rejection, smile, and keep on keeping on. I said, "Thank you," and was on my way. One down, one to go.

The first agent rejected me because I walked in with a really bad version of a homemade demo tape. I didn't take the time to use a stereo; I put my voice down on a cheap little recorder and just read from magazines. Even then, though, you could hear an interesting quality. The other problem was that there were virtually no voice-over agents or people doing them so it was hard to know where to look. At that time, I was told by someone at an ad agency "Just put your voice down on a tape and bring it to them." You need to remember we are talking about a small town that doesn't do a whole lot of voice-over work. On the same note, it was a wonderful place to hone my skills, begin a career and get some local, regional and national voice-over jobs. There is voice-over work everywhere and now when I visit Kansas City, I see that the same people are still in the business and making great money. The first agent I went to when I started in voice-overs was also an actor and represented himself. I called him, got an appointment and walked in with the tape in my hand. Unfortunately, he didn't send me on my way with any recommendations or advice.

On the tape, I put five or six different commercials from magazine ads in a row, on the tape. I would record one, push stop, then record another. I put the entire commercial on the tape and thought I was on my way. I tried to pick out commercials where I saw products I thought I could sell. At that point, I decided to make copies of the tape and send it to local production houses and advertising agencies.

Tapes that are sent without agent representation are called unsolicited tapes. They can be mailed to anyone you want to listen to your tape. Send them to people who could potentially hire you for a job: radio stations, schools, advertising agencies, theaters, production companies, post production facilities, trailer companies, loop groups, audio books, casting houses, animation companies, even the Internet. Unsolicited tapes can be sent everywhere you want your voice to be. Put your name and phone number on the tape; include a cover letter and send out the tape. Make a call first to find out who is in charge of the voice-over division, or to whom to send a note and tape. Someone doesn't necessarily have to know you or your voice to listen to a tape. You have to start somewhere. A demo tape may get thrown away without being listened to, but then they may pop it in and listen! That's why you have to make a lot of copies.

I only made about five copies of the tape when I started, but it was enough to keep me concentrated and motivated.

Fake tapes are commonly used when voice-over actors don't have any real tape. A fake tape is made by taking ads from anywhere you can find them or pulling them from actual copy on TV or radio and recording it onto the tape with your voice. Your tape is your signature, like a business card. Rarely, unless it's a big national spot by a famous celebrity, will the person listening to your tape even know it's not a real spot. You won't have the spot as well edited (music, cues) as you would with the real tape being produced in a sound studio, but you only want the person(s) listening to get a "feel" for the attitude that you are projecting. A tape shouldn't be longer than two to three minutes. Also, the tape should have shorter spots with different attitudes, characters and personalities. The only time you should use an entire commercial, is when you are doing homemade tape. You won't have the luxury of editing, so just do your best reads and stick them in a row on the tape. Stop the tape at the end of each read, and resume recording when you are ready for the next read. Have other people listen to the tape before you send it out.

Your homemade demo tape should vary in style and reads. It's very important to move beyond that one read that features your deep, husky voice. Most people start in voice-overs because someone has told them they have a great voice. Then they take a class and realize it's a lot of acting work and the voice is secondary to reading copy. When you do the tape, make sure that you've varied your reads. Don't do a tape all the same way. Five or six commercials all the same texture, sexiness, inflection won't get anyone's attention. It is very important to practice, to study acting if you need to and listen to how people really sound on commercials. If you speak one way off mike, and another on, you will need to learn to relax and get comfy with the microphone. Your reads, while taking into account what the advertiser is looking for, should somewhat be within your natural vocal range. Creating characters is something different. Learn to play with your own voice to find different attitudes and natural adjustments. This will open up your reads, allow the action to take place and keep you from "pushing," letting the flow of the work come naturally instead of "working" your voice. You will learn to use your voice as simply the tool to relay the message of the product.

Using acting as a tool will change the way in which you "sell" each commercial. You will be amazed at how many different tones and textures come out of your voice when you begin to tell a story. Instead of worrying about the words on the paper, start learning how to deliver them.

I looked through the yellow pages for the addresses and found about four production houses. I called the local junior college and dropped off a tape for the drama department. I also gave a tape to the few local radio stations. I got my first job a few weeks later. A local spot, but great fun. The production company was run by a one-man operation. I got paid $50.00 under the table (non-union) and was done.

"Under the table" is a term widely used in the voice-over industry for jobs that aren't union. Non-union work is legal. Smaller companies and companies that don't want an inflated budget or don't have the funds, will use non-union talent. Generally, they can get non-union talent cheaper. Non-union talent works with the producer/writer/director to agree upon a fee between the parties. This can be as little as a copy of the tape and gas money. It depends upon what you decide. There is no set fee, thus it is called non-union. You cannot work "under the table" if you are in the union. You can be fined, suspended, or released from the union if you are caught.

I was on my way! From that first radio job, I booked more. They called me in a lot and other people in town heard my voice and started calling. Some jobs I did for free, and others I was paid a small (under the table) fee. The radio station pulled me in for a promo and that was the beginning. I got the other agent in town to take me on, and eventually got a better tape made, using the real work that I had been doing, mixed with a few "fakes."

Eventually, voice-overs became my day job!

I got industrial films, in-house videos for local and regional stores, and all sorts of work.

The ad agencies, NO MATTER WHERE YOU LIVE, do regional, local and national campaigns. This means that you can book jobs wherever you are. This is the point. There is work out there; you just need to know how to find it. Then, you just need to do it. I moved to Los Angeles in 1987 with 25 demo tapes in hand, looking for an on-camera career.

At first, I had to support myself waitressing and working for a famous talent agency. I worked 12-hour days and tried to fit in auditions when I could get away. I tried to work my hours so I would be available during audition times, which could be anywhere from nine in the morning to six at night.

What I got was much better. I sent the tapes around, landed an agent (pocketed, I wasn't in a union yet). They sent me out on auditions, and two weeks later I landed a national commercial. This put me in the union and the rest, as they say, is history. I started from local radio to bigger radio to TV to advertising campaigns.

I remember thinking, "If I could just get a radio spot," and then, "If I could only get a TV spot," and "If I could only get a national commercial," and, "If I could only get a campaign," to "IF I could only get an animated series." It's never-ending. But it's nice to see your goals achieved. At one time, I've had as many as 20 national commercials running, and I still want more. You never stop wanting to succeed. It is attainable. But you cannot leave it to someone else to do it for you, and you can't use the excuse that you don't know what to do. I'm going to help you through it.

Hopefully, I'll start you on the right track and save you a lot of time. Good luck on your voice-over journey! I'm loving mine.

—Terri Apple

CHAPTER 1

• • •

WHAT IS A VOICE-OVER?

• • •

As defined in *Webster's Dictionary*, a voice-over is "the voice commenting or narrating off camera, as for a television commercial."

These voices are selling products on the radio or television and you are buying them! Yes, voice-overs are the jingles that you sing in the shower and can't remember why, and they're the little buzz words that you say at odd times of the day because the advertiser has drilled them into your head 70 times a day . . . "Coke is it," "Get your burger's worth," "Got milk?" and these voice-over actors are making a fortune!

The main union and guild covering voice-over artists, AFTRA/ American Federation Of Television and Radio Artists, defines a voice-over performer as someone who reads copy and is not seen on-camera. Voice-overs on radio and television commercials are considered to be anything up to three minutes in length. Anything over three minutes is considered voice-over narration.

On television shows, it's the voice that you hear while watching action going on. If you hear the person speaking while on-camera, that is not a voice-over. (Don't confuse voice-overs with "dubbing." Dubbing is putting your voice in place of another person's.)

Voice-overs are also the voices you hear in animation (Saturday morning cartoons as well as feature-length films), audio books, industrial films, infomercials, trailers in the movies, tag lines on commercials, promotional spots, and so forth.

Are you still interested? Then ask yourself two questions:

1. How's my voice?
2. Can I act?

A good and interesting voice will help, as it makes people remember you and what you are selling. I refer to it as "the icing on the cake." But having a good voice isn't everything. You also need to know how to act. Getting in front of a mike, saying the copy with the right delivery (the one the client wants) and making it all come in at the precise length required (and keep this up for many takes) is not as simple as it seems. However, there are some insider tips and tricks that I will teach you. So, keep reading.

PERSONALITY, ATTITUDE AND CHARACTER

Personality, attitude and character are more important than having a deep or high-pitched voice. It is very important to have the tool (your voice) but you need to know how to use that tool.

Personality is the way in which you read the copy, putting your unique character or flair into the read. If you can act, it helps. It will keep you fresh and different every time you read. Personality is your trademark—what makes your voice stand out from the competition.

How you define yourself as a person correlates to how you read copy. Your normal rhythms, natural sound and vocal quality will come through. This is your starting point. It is important to define your "signature" voice—the one you feel most comfortable using. How do you sound when you meet someone? How about when you meet someone you are excited about meeting? Unhappy about meeting? Does your voice go up when you become excited? Uncomfortable? What about when you are lonely or sad? Does your voice change? What about when you are in a fight in a restaurant with someone as opposed to the privacy of your home? How about with whom you are fighting? Doesn't your voice change? Doesn't it change the way in which you say certain words?

These are all qualities that are an important part of your personality. Bring them with you to your read. The only difference between you and several hundred others reading for the same job, is your personality. You may be able to copy someone's voice, but you cannot copy their personality. It will sound stilted and forced. That is why the best thing that you can bring to a read in order to get the job, is your own, unique take on the commercial. This is within reason, of course. It depends on what the advertiser is looking for. For example, they may be looking for an upbeat, fun dad. That still leaves the door open for interpretation, doesn't it? There are so many different dads out there. Age, ethnicity, energy, education—any of these may or may not be defined on the copy. It may be up to you to "find" the right read for the spot.

Once you get used to reading copy and relaxing into it, the

reads will come a lot more smoothly and naturally. Everyone has his or her own natural rhythms and inflections. As well as the rhythms written into the copy. You will learn to find these as you read, practice and book jobs. It is important to play around with your own voice, then see where it can take you.

Attitude: The emotion or feeling that the copy dictates or that you bring to the read. Are you friendly? Arrogant? Lazy? Ditzy? Excited? Complacent?

Equally important to personality is attitude. This is the core of the read. How are you selling the spot? What feeling are you bringing to the read? Who are you selling to? Ask these questions. How am I feeling? (through what the copy says and how it says it) How is your mood? Edgy? Off the cuff? Matter of fact? Businesslike? Intimate? Who are you selling to? Girl Scouts? Young pregnant mothers? Health care patients? Attitude is what you have to go on to give yourself a base to begin the read. Otherwise, you may sound too general, like you're not speaking to anyone in particular. If I know that I'm going to read for 7-UP and I need to sound hip, cool and detached (according to the description on the copy) then I know that I should use those qualities within my personality. My attitude should follow what they are looking for.

Character: Who is the advertiser trying to reach? How are they saying it, and to what specific audience?

Character defines the above and more. Attitude and personality are the specific version of character. Your character is the overall persona that you are projecting into the read. Sometimes your character is nothing at all but being yourself and putting it into the read. Character comes up a lot more for animation when you really spend more time trying to come up with specific voices to fit the character you are playing. I think that equally important is coming up with character within yourself to fit the reads of regular commercials for television and radio. The difference is that you don't change your voice as much. You change your personality and mood. Don't get confused when you need to have "character" voices for regular commercials. Character can simply mean using your personality to change a reads attitude. Change of character can mean just a tweak in your voice or a change in stance at the microphone. It's a way to say something differently. Start adding a whole new range of styles to help enhance your chance of getting jobs.

Why Do I Want a Voice-over Career?

- You can escape from the routine nine to five job.
- You get to act.
- You get to create voices that normally only your pet would hear.
- You are part of a creative process in a multi-million dollar industry.
- You get paid for having fun!

Voice-overs are for people with personality, flexible voices and acting skills. They are not, however, for those who are lazy or faint of heart. It is very difficult to keep bringing in money on a regular basis unless you've built a clientele and are working steadily. This career is cyclical: some months are better than others. You may be the hot commodity for a year and then have a dreadful year the next. It's just the nature of the business. Advertisers change their minds. They go with different sounds all the time. They may want to change in order to bring in a different type of audience.

No matter how talented you are or how well you read the copy, you still may not book the job. Knowing how to interpret the copy and read according to direction is what clients and casting directors look for. If you don't book the job after doing what was your best audition in the world, you may never know why. More than likely, the client wanted another style of voice, and you don't know what any other voice-over artist did in their read. Don't spend too much time worrying about why you didn't get the last job. Move on to the next one.

Start-Up Costs

Start up costs for voice-over careers vary. There is one common goal: to get work. How do you get the work? Through classes, talent and a demo tape. Voice-over/Animation classes can run you anywhere from $39.00 for a one day-seminar at the Learning Annex to ongoing classes that teach you everything from how to breathe, how to work the microphone, how to interpret copy, and how to work with your voice to how to book the job.

Costs for these classes can run anywhere from $100 to $500. Find out the best prices for the kind of class that you are looking for. Ask around. Ask agents, teachers, and fellow actors. Find out the best class in that town for what you want to do and the amount of money you can spend. Quite a few casting directors, producers and even other voice-over actors offer classes and even produce tapes.

Don't spend your money to have a tape professionally produced unless you are ready. By ready, I mean that you can use a microphone and give a natural sounding read. You should be comfortable with your read and not feel the need to re-do each read 15 times. You have learned characters and interpretations of reads and know how to read and how to act on the microphone.

When preparing your tapes, keep each kind of voice-over on a separate tape. Commercials on your commercial tape, promo/narration on your narration tape, animation on your animation tape, etc.

Your main start up costs will be for classes to learn basic skills. Having a great voice isn't enough. Learning what to do with that voice is the key to a long and lucrative career. If you make a demo tape without training, you are taking a chance of having your work not seen in a great light. Hold off making that tape (homemade or produced) until you have taken a class (or two, or three). If you've already got a demo tape, bring it to the class. Let the teacher listen to it, before you continue sending it out.

A produced demo tape can cost from $300 to $700 depending on if you've hired a director/producer to work with you. You will also have to pay the studio where you produce your tape.

It's very important to use whatever "tools" you have within you. Use your personality in the read. Don't "stifle " your personality when you get on the microphone. Too many people think they need to push (manipulate, enhance) a read or fake it while reading copy. All this does is keep you from sounding natural and conversational. It takes practice, classes, and experience to learn how to read copy and start to make it sound real.

Take a little break now and choose a piece of copy from the samples in Appendix A. Take a deep breath and pick a mood. Any mood. Invent or imagine a person to tell your story to (the copy) and read. As you read, read aloud as if you are sharing the story with that person. Make it real even though you are selling a product. Try each read several ways. Pick a different mood, choose different "people" to sell your product to. Try to decide what sort of vocal quality the advertiser will hire for the job.

BUILDING YOUR CAREER WHILE ENHANCING YOUR LIFE

What do I mean? Think about it! How much does a voice affect every way in which we interact with people? All over the United States, we see advertisements:

Enhance Your Voice.

Get What You Want!

Be A Leader. Speak Like A Leader!
The Way To Get What You Want Is Through Your Voice!
Speak With Confidence!
Using Your Voice As A Tool In How To Succeed!

To some extent the advice in these ads is true. Remember your grade school teacher that you laughed at because her voice was so nasal? Or the high school dweeb who couldn't raise his voice above a whisper? How about using your voice to your benefit? Who were the class leaders? How about football players? You don't hear any meek little voices there. Speakers, owners of companies, directors, anyone in a place of position knows to use his voice as a tool. Speaking is very important. Kathy Ireland, the model, had a very high squeaky voice. Her voice had to be dubbed. Eventually she took speaking and voice lessons and learned how to modulate her voice. People who once laughed at her now were eagerly listening to what she had to say. Who knows, perhaps it gave her the personal security to start her own bathing suit line. Changing her voice changed the way that Kathy Ireland saw herself and others saw her.

Andie McDowell, the actress, is another good example. Her voice was so poorly received by the producers, directors and anyone who saw her first movie that the studio hired Glenn Close to dub her lines. Andie McDowell's voice is sort of nasal, with a thick Southern accent. Glenn Close's voice was more commanding. Not all women should sound like a deep-throated woman of the 90's, but whatever your voice, you can learn to take control of it and speak with confidence.

How does this tie in with voice-overs?

In every way. Advertisers are always looking for something specific. Listen to the ads. They want young moms who can relate to young moms. How does one sound? Attitude? Style? Breathing?

Voices reflect attitudes. Selling a product is simply selling an attitude. Every piece of copy that you read has direction at the bottom. How else would you know what they want? You can pick your own attitude based on the product, how it's written and what is seen (for TV) but the copywriter already has an idea what he is looking for. A very high-pitched voice tends to "read" young, shy, unsure, naive, little boys, fun, over the top. A deep voice "reads" authoritative, in control, strong. An older, strong yet soft voice tends to "read" warm, trusting, loving, comforting.

The advertiser puts the voice (Attitude) into the kind of spot he is trying to sell to a particular market. You are much more apt to hear an older man or woman selling Tylenol, than a young, hip, surfer dude. That is, unless the copy is geared towards selling Tylenol to a surfer market. Why do you think Mountain Dew is geared toward a teenage market? They didn't stick Martin Sheen or Donald Sutherland in there, they're more apt to use Jonathan Taylor Thomas so that kids his age will listen. Even if they don't know that it's him, they can feel the age, the attitude, and they can relate.

Now, take a break. When you're ready, begin the next section and practice the exercises.

EXERCISES

Look through magazines for advertising copy, choose one to work with and try the following:

1. Read each ad aloud three different ways. What kind of read would it be? What is the advertiser trying to say? How would the commercial sell? To what age market? What type of person? Where is the tag in the spot? What do you think the important words or phrases are?
2. Record the spot. Read it aloud. Listen back. What would you do differently?
3. Choose and ad without copy (one that uses only a picture and a brand name)—what would you write for copy? What do you think they are selling? Take this opportunity to be creative. Read aloud. Record them. Play them back.

1.

CHAPTER 2

• • •
SO I'VE GOT A GREAT VOICE, NOW WHAT?
• • •

BREAKING INTO THE BUSINESS

To get your first job, you will have to audition. To audition, you have to know where they're being held. To do that, you have to know the casting directors (or rather, they have to know you and your work). Casting houses are listed in yellow pages. Call your local branch of the Screen Actors Guild (SAG) or American Federation of Radio and TV Artists (AFTRA) and ask for a list of casting directors. SAG and AFTRA are the two unions that will represent you as a voice-over artist. You can also call the Casting Society of America in Los Angeles. They sell lists of casting directors for an affordable price. (See Appendix for contact information)

There are several ways to find out about voice-over jobs. If you have an agent, your agent can submit you, or you can go after the jobs on your own through production companies, ad agencies and casting directors. Make that homemade tape and send it to local agencies, schools, industrial companies, looping houses, audiobook publishers and casting facilities. They will contact you when they have something for you to read. Try to establish relationships and build a clientele for your future.

PRACTICE! PRACTICE! PRACTICE!

Pick up a magazine, read a book aloud, watch TV, and listen! Listening is important. You need to hear what is selling, what people are listening to.

People often confuse being able to do voice-overs with being able to do voice imitations: "I can do a great Stallone;" "I can do a really good Swahili swordsmen." Only Sylvester Stallone would be hired to "do Stallone" and, do Swahili swordsmen even exist?

It's great that you can entertain your family and friends, but when it comes to the real world, listen! No one does ads for fake Swahilis, they are doing real ads with real people. Even in animation, they may call for a "Stallone-like" character. Then you can play with the accent and attitude and come up with a voice, or you can play with the Swahili and come up with a good character. In the real world of advertising, you very rarely need a good Swahili. Don't do caricatures.

Remember what we said about character, attitude and personality? Play with your voice a little to develop different attitudes and moods. To "play" with your voice try reading the commercials in a different manner each time. Take a short piece of copy and read it differently each time, using each of these individual words as the only direction given to you: Soft, loud, exuberant, deep, raspy, smooth, higher pitched, slower, faster, change the pace. Now, try some accents; make funny pitch noises with sentences. Go up on one ending and down on another. Stress certain words. Stress certain *parts* of the words. Get down and dirty with your voice. Do everything you can with the words and be as silly as you can be. Call your friends and disguise your voice. This is a great exercise to limber you up and get all those voices and personalities that exist in your repertoire of talent. Have some fun!

Now pick a few different characters for yourself and see what you can come up with. Be a smoldering sexpot, a dark, mysterious detective, a yuppie tennis player at a club, a gas station attendant with a bad haircut. Create these characters, figure out how they would sound based on their backgrounds and description as well as what they do and how they feel. Each character and mood will bring out a different inflection and speech pattern within your own voice.

No matter what town you live in, there are talent agencies, schools, radio stations, classes, college courses, Learning Annexes, advertising agencies and production facilities. This means that whatever town that you live in, you can work. You don't have to be in Hollywood, New York, or Chicago. These are the three major markets, but all the other states offer voice-overs, a lot of it non-union, which means less competition, and you have a better chance of booking jobs!

☞ *Don't forget to practice different voices around your house or in your car.*

How to Begin

Watch television commercials. See the kinds of things you would be right for, that you could see yourself doing. Imagine ways you, your personality and ability would be right for.

Study how actors sell the products. What kind of read is it? Is there anything unusual or interesting in the wording, the placement of the words? The design of the ad can tell you a lot about what the ad agency and client are trying to convey. What do they want us, the consumer, to feel, to see, to understand? Does the whole campaign fit together? Was it designed for teenagers, elders, or Harley-Davidson riders?

Listen to the radio. Hear what advertisers are selling. The voice-over is even more important here than on television, as it's the only selling tool. Pay attention to what kinds of voices are used more often. What makes you listen to a spot, or change the station? What vocal qualities do you enjoy, and sound familiar, share? Do they catch your ear? Would you remember the commercial or buy the product?

Write down the ad copy. Write the commercials down and practice reading them. Don't imitate, just follow the attitude. Try many different ways there would be to read the spot, and then you will begin to understand what the writer and agency were looking for and what made them go with the read that they did.

Record yourself. Get any recorder that you can find. Dust off your old one. This is just to play with. Now take the copy that you have written down and the copy that I have given you on the following pages and get to work. Be sure to use a microphone. For right now, depend on no technique other that what comes naturally for you. There are no "tricks." Later on we'll talk about stereotyping and what is selling, but for now, just play! After you've recorded the spot and done it a number of ways, listen back. You need to start getting comfortable any way you can. It's a good beginning. Listen to the way that you have said it. Listen to your tone, your breath, your timing, your pace. Time the commercial.

Soon you will be able to tell how long commercials ("spots") run. There are many different timings, and the only way to know how long the advertisers want the spot is to record the commercial from copy start to copy finish. This way you will know how long the spot is. Try to get it in that time. This will be helpful when you begin to audition. You need to start being able to get the read in the time they want.

•

Research

Besides sending out demo tapes, do as much research as you can about the business. Read books on diction and accents. Listen to tapes about speech patterns and dialects. Take as many acting, singing, dialect classes as you can afford.

☞ *Learn to relax. Your auditions and jobs will go a lot easier. Relaxation, meditation, hypnotherapy, yoga, these are all great ways to relax your body. Open up your lungs so you can speak longer without taking so many breaths. Work out. Cardiovascular fitness makes it easier to breathe and gives you better lung capacity to speak.*

I bought a recorder and diligently went through real ads in magazines and read aloud. I recorded myself. I tried to create as many moods as I could come up with by what the picture was and what the ad said. I drew cartoon characters, made up from my head and gave them names. Then I gave them distinct walks and mannerisms. This helped me find their voices. I would record everything and time it. If it was for a regular commercial I would time it so I would know specifically how long the spot was supposed to be. While I watched TV, I would write down and time the ad. Then I would read the spot and see if I could get it in that time. Knowing a commercial or ad helped me understand what that client and ad agency was looking for. It helped me know if I was in the right career. Could my voice be cast in that commercial? Your secret to doing voice-overs is that you make it sound real for yourself. If you believe the copy that you are reading aloud, then you will get an audience to believe it and buy it. That's what the ad agencies want; a unique voice that will help sell their product. You do that and you've got some happy customers!

Warm Ups and Cold Drinks

I don't use any warm up exercises, though many other voice-over professionals deep breathe, visualize restful places, or use other relaxing techniques. As for quenching your thirst and getting your voice ready, cold water is the best thing you can drink. Soda constricts the muscles in your throat and makes you burp; avoid bubbles. Water is soothing. Tea is good for sore throats and so is honey, but warm temperatures can constrict muscles and can make your voice deeper and raspier.

OTHER AVENUES OF EMPLOYMENT

While you are improving your voice and copy reading, you might want to call production companies that specialize in documentaries. You can even try your local mall and see about doing the intercom announcements. Widen your horizon of choices. If you can't send a tape or don't have one, go another route until you do.

DIFFERENT KINDS OF READS

There are so many different types of reads that it would be virtually impossible to name them all. Any style or range of your voice that you can come up with, qualifies as a valid read. If you want to stand on your head and speak in a high pitched voice while trying to whistle, go for it, although I'm not sure you'll be very comfortable doing it. Whatever is comfortable for you while you're reading is okay. Crossing your arms to emphasize a point, standing with your legs spread apart, toes crossed, lips clenched. Your hands high above your head. Play around with stance, rhythm, voice and speech pattern. Interestingly, the way that you stand, the manner in which you hold you hands, your head, your body, will directly sway your read.

> *When I was doing the campaign for HomeBase, (a chain of houseware stores) I found that I would stand hunched over holding onto a pencil when I did the read. It was a flat, monotone, character and I didn't even realize that standing that way. Once I became aware of that, I couldn't do the commercials without holding a pencil in my hand and standing in that position. I tried to sit and read the copy, to no avail. It wasn't the same. I had conditioned my body, voice and mind to believe that this stance was best suited for the character.*

Certain reads lend themselves to standing certain ways. If you are yelling off microphone (to give the feeling you are in another room or across the street) you will want to stand further from the microphone than you would normally. The same can be said of an intimate read. Stand very close to the microphone and speak softly. Play around with these characters that you do on the microphone and see how you are standing and/or sitting while you're reading. See how many stances you can come up with. Try standing different ways with the same characters and see if anything new comes up. Changes in accents, speed, inflection and rhythm can bring out your natural ability to create new and exciting voices.

This holds true for animation as well as commercials. Animation is really just a bigger form of characters than commercials. Commercials are more reality-based, so we say that the characters are coming from mood and personality whereas animation is created more from different places in our voice to give each character a distinct sound.

LISTEN TO HOW YOU SOUND

Most people think that they know what their voice sounds like, and then are shocked when they hear. Are you nasal? Are you stuttering? Breathing all over the place? Not coming across like you are talking to anyone? Sound like you're "just reading the copy?" All these are helpful in understanding the world of advertising.

TALK TO SOMEONE

When you are recording, pretend you are talking to someone. Your mother, father, sister, boyfriend, girlfriend, wife, police officer—whatever seems appropriate for the copy. Personalize your copy. This is very important. Doesn't it always seem like the voice-over person is just talking specifically to you? That's a secret to reads that work. Keep real. Be honest.

NARRATION/PROMO/ANIMATION

For narration, practice by reading advertising copy as well magazine or newspaper articles. Tape documentaries and shows on television and then write down the copy so you can practice reading it. Talk to whomever is in charge of hiring at local production or post-production facilities. Ask about any future documentary or narration work. Leave a demo tape. (Make sure it has narration work on it.) Doing the narration or voice-over for industrial films is another great way to get started in the narration and promo field.

For promos, write down (or tape and then write down) the short phrases, sentences that you hear promotion upcoming television and radio shows. (Fire on the freeway! News at eleven.)

The same advice goes for animation. Create characters. Draw them out if you've made them up. Think about what they would say and how they would say it. Make an animation tape that way.

Doing all sorts of different voices. Have them talk to each other if you want or tell a story, each one weaving through the next character. Watch animated TV shows to see what kind of voices are out there and what your competition will be like. The best way to find voices within your range is to play. Remember when you were a kid and would be different people? That's what you can do. No limits.

Animation classes will teach you how to create voices within yourself and how to get them from your body through the microphone. In order to pursue animation, you need to live in a city where they cast those types of jobs. In smaller markets, it would be best to concentrate on commercial voice-overs and narration. There is a lot more work in these areas.

DIFFERENT VOICES

Each of these words could be your direction for reading copy. They allow you to "create" different types of reads.

Tired	Cool
Sad	Cocky
Hungry	Relaxed
Angry	Perplexed
Flirty	Soft
Funny	Creative
Despondent	Shy
Wry	Edgy
Overwrought	Annoyed
Sardonic	Sarcastic
Overworked	Quiet
Bored	Loud
Animosity	Obnoxious
Turbulence	Braggart
Worried	Anxious
Tense	Forbidden
Fidgety	Mysterious
Apprehensive	Chivalrous
Loose	Dimwitted
Confused	Challenged
Weathered	Nervous
Drained	Cold
Sexy	Hot
Energetic	Sore

Feverish
Manipulating
Manipulated
Victimized
Controlling
Controlled
Frumpy
Silly
Sloppy
Elegant
Sophisticated
Boorish
Sympathetic
Overpaid
Underpaid
Empathetic
Candid
Raunchy
Remorseful
Playful
Careless
Careful
Motherly
Warm
Fatherly
Brotherly

Sisterly
Babyish
Grandmotherly
Grandfatherly
Teacherly
Disciplinarian
Antagonistic
Hedonistic
Sunburn
Rushed
Achy
Heavenly
Guilty
Protective
Lost
Subtle
Harassing
Pushy
Controversial
Timid
Bold
Nasal
Uppercrust
Deep-Voiced
Raspy
Smooth

PHYSICAL ATTRIBUTES

Physical attributes affect others aspects of your read. By changing your position at the microphone, you can change your state of mind. Adding one of the physical acts below to one or more of the emotional cues above will start you on your way to building a "character repertoire." OK, now here are some different physical ways to read:

Fingers Crossed
Toes Crossed
Closing Your Eyes
Blowing Your Nose
Stuffy Nose
Holding Your Nose

Talking Through Your Nose
Sitting In A Chair Legs Apart
Sitting In A Chair Legs Crossed
Sitting In A Chair Legs Crossed Indian Style
Laying Down
Laying On Your Stomach
Twisting Your Body Around
Arms Above The Head
Arms Crossed In Front Of You
Speaking With Accents: Australian, English, Southern, French
Higher Pitched
Lower Pitched
Standing At Different Places On The Microphone
Pulling Your Hair Tightly Around Your Head
Letting It Loose
Putting Your Hands In/Out of Your Pockets
Project Way Out
Stick Your Stomach Out As You Speak
Hold Your Breath, Then Speak As You Let Out
Talk While Out Of Breath
Hold Your Tongue Out And Speak.
Change Your Pitch In Your Throat By Screaming
Laughing
Yelling
Crying
Change Your Octave In Your Voice
Hands Behind Your Back
Short Sleeve Loose Shirt
Tight Top
One Arm On Your Hip Yelling
One Arm On Your Hip Talking Through Your Diaphragm
Trying To Move Your Ears While You Speak
Trying Not To Move Your Lips
Move Your Nose Up And Down
Batting Your Eyes

EXERCISE

Now try combining these. Take an attribute from the "Emotion" list
and combine it with another from the "Physical" list. Next, try using two attributes from one list and one from the other—mix it up
and see what voices you can find!

REAL LIFE VS. REEL LIFE

When you are speaking in your everyday life, you make these move-ments and changes very naturally, without noticing. Your voice will rise or fall by an octave depending on your mood. You use different voices to stress a point, to relax, to talk on the phone. These are all different characters within your voice that will help immensely when you are trying understand and read copy. The big difference here though, is that you don't pre-plan your voices in real life; you won't remember which response got you to speak or use the inflection you did when you excitedly jumped up and down and said, "Oh, my gosh!" If you were tired and lying down on the couch deliver-ing those same lines, it would sound completely different.

Our moods and emotions have great impact on how we "de-liver our lines" in real life. It is the only way other people know what we are feeling. Ever notice when you ask someone, "How are you?" and they come back with a terse, "Fine?" that you instinc-tively know they are *not* fine. You can "read" that they are upset. This is the way in which we learn to interpret voice-over copy and do great reads.

When you are auditioning or doing the actual voice-over ses-sion, you usually have a very small space in which to read. There is a microphone, a stand and a chair if you need it, and you! You will be limited in how much you can move around. Take those large movements we worked on and condense them; make them work for you in a smaller space. The tricky part is doing it physically smaller while still "selling your read"—making what you are say-ing sound real.

Now, read some of the sample copy in Appendix A again. Look at the direction at the bottom of the copy or make up your own. Decide what you think the mood should be. Pick one thing from every list and go for it. Now go back and pick a few things from all three lists. See? It's like building a house. Layer upon layer, upon layer. It's exactly what will happen in a session. You will be told to add more of "this" and take away some of "that" in order to get to the "perfect" read—the heart of the commercial.

EXERCISES

Look at the sample ads in Appendix A. Read them. Study them. Record them. Try to match the "feeling" of the spot. Interpret what the spot is trying to say. At the bottom of the audition copy, there will be some words of direction to guide you in your interpretation. All spots have an emotional base—basically the mood the advertiser is trying to create. It is the job of the advertiser to write the copy so that we, as the actors, can translate what they are trying to say, from the paper to television or radio.

For each ad, ask yourself the following questions:

- What is the advertiser saying in the visual? In the words?
- How are they trying to make me feel: Sensual? Sad? Worried? Business minded?
- How many different ways can I interpret this ad?
- How many different words can I push or pull back on?
- What would the timing on the ad be?
- What kind of person are they marketing? Selling to?

Pick three different types of reads for each spot. Record them.

> *"I feel like someone has it when they look at the copy like a piece of music and there is a rhythm to it. Voice quality is important but not as much as rhythm. It's all about rhythm. Students need to have a strong sense of who they are, personality needs to come through the mike. Know your niche!"*
> *—Marla Kirbin, in-house director, ICM, coach/teacher*

CHAPTER 3

• • •

FINDING YOUR TECHNIQUE

• • •

Everyone always asks me if I have a technique. I really don't. I don't breathe in a certain way, try to push a certain rhythm or make sure I read the copy the exact same way every time. What I do is ACT! I make sure every piece of copy is real for me, and that every piece of dialogue comes across as if I'm truly speaking to someone. It doesn't sound "forced" or "pushed." When you try to hard to work on aspects of dialogue instead of the emotional story of what is being said, you will find you get lost in the words instead of the story.

In order to use your voice appropriately, you have to use your personality. How? Read the copy/script through. Is it funny? Is it serious? Is there room for your own personality to come through? Is the copy written so that when you read it, it comes across naturally? A lot of times, copy is not written well—a sad fact. You may find it difficult to say lines that don't feel like something you'd say. That's where your acting ability comes in. You must be able to make the copy sound real, whether you are selling a product or acting a part you know nothing about.

So, we are *not* starting with the voice. We are working from the inside out; thus the icing on the cake theory. So what if you've got a great voice! (Not that I'm taking anything away from a wonderful, delicious, meltingly sensual voice, or a fun, quirky, weird, high pitched tone.) But do you know how to use it? Do you know how to sell the product using aspects of your voice? How to be able to sell that product to an audience without sounding like you're reading copy is where you can utilize your own special technique—and make the big bucks!

Read the copy the way the writer intended it. Every script has a natural rhythm and is trying to tell a story, even if it doesn't make sense to you. Every script is written with a purpose, no matter how silly or serious it may be.

When you over-analyze the script you can lose the meaning. Bring your personality and attitude to your read. It is your job as the voice-over actor to bring the "life" to the script. The writer hears it a certain way in his head. You will read it and make it real. That doesn't mean that the writer still doesn't believe how they want something said. If they hear the sentence a certain way, you will need to give them that read. When auditioning, you won't always know how the writer intended the copy to be read. You may not get the job simply because another actor read the copy the way the writer envisioned. This is all part of the business; you can't read minds, you just need to learn to follow your own instincts and rhythms.

Rule No. 1: Imagine you are speaking to a real person.
This will give you a point of view and allow your personality to shine through, making the read "real," no matter how brilliant (or boring) the copy is. It will also tend to relax you and give you a greater sense of control over your read.

Rule No. 2: Breathe
But not in the middle of words. After reading the copy a few times (silently as well as out loud so that it feels comfortable and natural), find comfortable points to exhale and inhale. Some copy is written so that you don't have much time to breathe. A lot of scripts are written with run-on sentences. You may read something and wonder, "How am I going to get through that sentence?" Breathing is the most important thing in a read. If you're short of breath (unintentionally) or not breathing in the right places, you will have trouble conveying the message of the script. The only time when being short of breath works is when you are reading a character in a script that is short of breath.

The more you practice, the more breathing will become second nature instead of an obstacle to overcome. If I'm being a character in the read, I don't have time to remember or ask myself when I need to breathe. That comes at the proper time. Think about when you breathe in everyday life. You certainly don't pay attention and say to yourself, "Oh yeah, I better breathe now." Same thing in voice-overs. It just feels more complicated and obvious to you because you are putting all of your energy into speaking. You are standing in front of a microphone, saying words with a headphone on, which creates anxiety because your entire focus is on how you are going to say something. Worry less about how you are going to say it and more on what you are saying. As long as you are in the moment, explaining (talking) to the audience or relaying to them your story (script/copy) you can't lose. You will make every read the best they could possibly read. An ad executive may not hire you, but they may say, "I love the way that person interpreted the copy; no one else did it like that." That's what makes you unique!

Rule No. 3: Find a technique or way to read the copy that works for you.

My name and voice are known for a certain style of read that is very flat and quirky. That is only one style and I do many more. Develop your own style and technique—whatever works for you. Never copy another voice-over actor; instead create and develop your own inner voice and strength.

> When I started taking acting classes, there were so many different ways in which to learn. Some classes believed in "method" (where you re-create past history of events and bring it into current situations). Others work strictly from the written word and do objectives (Laugh here. Cry here. Yell on this line. Be annoyed on that line.) Some classes are much more mechanical, others technical, others natural, even surreal. Bring forth what works for you. I cannot tell you not to study or to learn a certain way. But if you've never picked up a script or done a voice-over before, I can tell you which way is easy and works.
>
> My background is method training. Do I use it in my voice-over work? Absolutely. The difference is, I'm seen and not heard. The commercial copy sometimes is a little less dramatic than doing a scene from Tolstoy or Chekhov. But the main idea is the same. Whatever you are acting or interpreting has to come from reality, no matter if the copy is about fire safety, Coors Beer, Ford Trucks or Chevy Suburbans, Toys For Tots, McDonalds, AIDS research, cancer, leukemia or Barbie's Summer Corvette, or any of thousands of other products.

Your ability to incorporate your individual style into each read is extremely important. It's pretty easy to copy someone else's style or read, but would be the point? Do we all want to be clones of one another? I'm sure that in a way, it seems that when you watch TV or listen to the radio, you are hearing voices that sound similar.

Once a voice or style of voice becomes popular, clients of other products want to use a similar voice. They feel that this will help their product sell. Even if voices sound similar, there are general differences. The differences are how we say certain words, the ability to interpret copy in a different way from ten other people reading the same script, and our own personality.

> *When I started out, I did not intentionally seek out to have a certain trend or style of a voice. I still do not see my work as, "Oh, she does that flat read." I can absolutely do that flat read as well as several other types of reads, depending on the copy. I can be high energy, funny, sardonic, witty, warm, supportive, energetic and several other thousand ways. Get my drift? Reading is a lot like living life. The one thing you have to do is be able to evoke those emotions and bring them to the read.*

HUMOR

Humor is important when you are saying dialogue. You need to find humor (and there may not be any) within the dialogue and where it is. Make sure that you use it, if it's fitting for the spot. I don't mean you should laugh throughout the spot. I mean put a touch of humor, a smile, an irreverance to the read. Anything quirky, offbeat, or fun. Humor is one of the ways we see things in life. Within humor, there are still choices to make—ironic? subtle? abrasive? childish?—these are only a few of the different options, and they all affect your read and the way you are selling the product.

GRASP OF LANGUAGE

Learn to interpret the way in which something is written. What did the writer mean when they wrote that particular line or phrase? Understanding the language in the world in which we live and being able to speak it properly is very important in the world of voiceovers. You are representing a product, through speech. Having a grasp of the language you are speaking is very important. Correct pronunciation of words is a must. If you pronounce certain words or syllables differently from other people, study and learn to change that. If you have a strange speech pattern or a lisp, you're going to need to correct this problem. See a speech pathologist or take a diction class to work on your enunciation and speech patterns.

All languages have a natural rhythm or fluidity to them. French people seem to come across more passionately. Americans may be a little more casual while the English may have a more proper, formal sound. If you were to do voice-overs in other countries, you would need to learn a way to pick up on their inflection of certain words, the humor they use, and the way in which the say certain phrases. Just as important is the way in which they end certain words, depending on which part of that country they live. Accents and tones have a lot to do with it. Many midwesterners have very obvious twang. I get told I have a regional sound to my voice. I believe it's in my natural rhythm in which I say certain words, which of course has to do with where I was raised and the way I was taught to enunciate certain words. Do you say Tah-may-to? or Tah-mah-to? Different regions have different names for the same product. Sack or bag? Soda or Coke? Pocket book or purse? Do you "stand in line" or "stand on line?" Every city or region has different words and different ways in which words are spoken and pronounced.

In advertising, the verbal language is the same. You will not hear incorrect use of the literary language. You will not hear any fumbling of words or phrases unless it's deliberate. When we hear commercials on TV or radio, no matter how different we all may be, we can relate to what they are selling. Ad agencies will use the simplest form available to sell you (the public) their product, no matter if you live in South Central Los Angeles; Brooklyn, New York; Beverly Hills, California or Atlanta, Georgia. They still want to come across with a general message, "BUY THIS PRODUCT." Everyone has his own language among friends, groups, communities and even towns. Yet, the reason advertising stays so middle of the road is so everyone will understand what they are selling, no matter where they live.

INTERPRETATION OF CHARACTER

When you get copy to read, there will be a basic direction that tells you about the character the client is looking for. The way you read the dialogue and assess how this copy should be read, is from your interpretation or way in which you see the script.

For example, a radio script may say: "Girl next door, friendly, upbeat, late 20's."

Everyone can interpret this differently. This interpretation of this girl, is what makes 20 people, give twenty different reads. You will not have a writer, director or casting person tell you exactly how to do a read.

Let me give you a further example of copy for the girl next door, friendly, upbeat, late 20's:

"I was having coffee with Beth, when the phone rang. It was Sue. She's yelling into the phone, 'JC PENNY is having a half-off sale. Wanna go?' So, I'm thinking, are you out of your mind? See you in five."

Even within knowing age of the girl and basic personality traits, there are so many other things you can create. Who's Sue to you? Do you gossip with Beth? Are you excited and talking fast? Are you thinking about what Sue is telling you and then waiting to respond while you're reading the copy? Or, are you reading the copy as if you are relaying the story to another person, several days later?

All these things change a read. There is no wrong way. The only right way is the one the ad agency picks.

It's your job as the voice-over artist to bring life to this character. If you get the job, the character is going to become you. Any pauses, squeaking noises of excitement, sarcastic tones or emphasis on certain words, are up to you. When you get into the session, the writer/director will have certain words they want you to emphasize or change. But right now in the audition process, you don't have anyone holding your hand and telling you, word for word, which way to do something.

You have to be the one (as the voice-over actor) to decide how to say the lines, "I was having coffee with Beth." How do you want to say it? It's quite obvious with that line that she's just beginning to explain a story. You may decide to pause after, "with Beth." You may decide to emphasize coffee or I. Usually, once you have a grasp of the language for that particular spot, the dialogue will become natural to read. You won't be worrying about how to say each word, or whether to go up or down. If you're "in" the read (sounding like a real person) there are thousands of different interpretations you could have.

Take that same dialogue and make it a 16 year old boy. Let's say the character description says "teenage boy, laid back, surfer type, attitude."

See how much different the read will come out? Even if the words are the same, your interpretation of what you are saying will be different. Descriptions will change the entire mood of the read.

Let's try one more character description:

How about "Higher pitched woman in her 50's, working three jobs, tired, bored, witty."

Go back and read the copy. I'm sure you can come up with at least three reads or more that fit into this category and each read will have been different because you are working in the moment, telling the story, relating real emotion. If you're a man reading this, change the character to a man and try the same thing.

I understand you may think that there isn't anything at all "witty" in the read. That's not the point. You may not be able to know how to act like you've got three jobs. Descriptions can be tricky. The point is, the ad agency created them and the descriptions are the only way that convey what kind of voice and/or style of read they are looking for. You see how little voice quality comes into the read? They will most likely have one word about voice quality such as warm, older, raspy, wry, deep, high-pitched, quirky. The rest of the description will have absolutely NOTHING to do with your voice, but with your attitude and personality. This is why your interpretation of the character is so important.

DEPTH OF EMOTION: COPY, DIALOGUE AND CHARACTER

In addition to your personality and vocal characteristics, your emotions affect the read. The writer/director will tell you what they want in the read. Here are a few emotional descriptions that have come from advertising copy: sad, happy, enticed, empathetic, nurturing, caring, wise, strong, witty, charming, detached, rude, tired, bored, warm, hostile, aggressive, assertive, irreverent, reverent, sexy, snobby, slow, energized, hyper, maudlin.

Get the idea? There are so many ways of being. The depth of being is another matter. How far should you go with your emotion? It depends on what the writer/director wants for the copy. You don't want to over-emote. Keep it real! Overacting is putting too much emphasis on words and dialogue. Being too snobby, too bitchy, too sad, without also being enticing, witty or charming. Try putting a few emotions together and see what you get. How about trying certain emotions with this line below:

Isn't the moon beautiful?

Now, try this sad and sexy. How about aggressive and hyper? Okay, what about sardonic and wry?

Here are some more emotions and characteristics that ad agencies frequently use in their copy.

Wry-sarcastic, friendly, upbeat, casual, relaxed, flat-monotone, business read-straight forward informative, irreverent-like you don't care, off the cuff or thrown away-don't push the words or emphasize them so much, keep it simple, dry-sarcastic, witty, funny, sharp, informative, elderly, business-like.

These are just a few examples, but I want you to understand different depths and emotional levels. Something can be read business-like but witty. They don't cancel each other out. This means that you should read the copy intelligently and informatively, but give it some wit. Make it fun. Just because a read has information doesn't mean it can't be funny as well. A read can also be raspy and sarcastic. The rasp is just in your natural sounds and the sarcastic is how you sell the copy. They can ask for raspy sexy, smooth sexy or high pitched sexy. All three of these reads will come out sounding differently. Three different emotions. Three different depths. Each one can be pushed or pulled back (made stronger or weaker in tone, character and level). If they say smooth sexy, take away the rasp. They want a smoother, softer, read. They may also say, "Smooth it out." This is a technical term for evening out the words as they form in your mouth. You may be making the read too "Choppy." This means you're breaking up the words too much. The story isn't sounding like it's flowing together.

We have the technical components and the emotional components. Then we have your voice. Together these form a commercial.

PHRASING OF WORDS

There are several ways to look at the phrasing of words. Half of it is noting how the writer wrote the copy down on the actual page of dialogue you are reading. There will be a certain way that the writer has phrased the dialogue. Certain sentences may stand out, or a phrase may be followed by three dots, indicating a pause. It is the same general use of the language we are taught. How about this:

Isn't the moon beautiful tonight?

Take your different direction from the writer, your emotion, your interpretation of character, and let's add some punctuation and see what happens to the way that you read the copy:

Isn't the moon beautiful . . . tonight?

or;

*Isn't the
moon beautiful tonight?*

or;

Isn't the. . . moon, beautiful.   Tonight?

Doesn't this change around the read? Ad copywriters do this on purpose. They want you to read it that way. Now, here's the tricky part. Sometimes it's written a certain way because they are technically trying to get timings for the copy and they didn't take the time to re-write it before they sent it out for you to audition. Your only job should be to read the copy and see that it makes sense the way it's written. If it seems confusing to you, ask the casting director if they think that the writer intentionally wrote the copy that way. The casting director can be a big help. When you get in the session, after you've booked the job, you can ask the director if they want the dialogue read in the phrasing that it's written or if you should do your own phrasing.

Often, there will be a natural phrasing of words after you've studied the copy and read it aloud. There will be a rhythm of the phrasing that will come to you from saying certain words. If it helps you to pre-plan certain phrases that you find funny or interesting, and you think they should stand out a little more than others, then say them. That is what makes your read different.

☞ *Always make sure you enunciate the name of the product. Don't make it so obvious that it sounds like you are trying to push the product down the listener's throat, just make sure that you don't rush right through the product name. Take your time with the copy. Play around with it. Have fun! Relax, take a deep breath, and read!*

Presentation of the Copy

The way in which the copy is written or typed, typefaces, bold, italics, color, etc., all will affect the way you react to it. There are so many aspects to voice-overs. From the written copy to the spoken word. The choice of typeface or font can tell you a great deal about how they want you to feel when reading the advertisement. Fonts are used to project a certain sell. **Bold face type** is used to stress certain words that we should take more seriously. *Words in italics* will give a feeling of delicacy or secrecy. Small type gives you the feeling of a more intimate conversation read, while ALL CAPS makes you feel like you should be broader with the copy.

Writers and ad agencies write the copy, especially for advertisements (billboards, signs, restaurant logos) to be seen. They put a lot of thought into how you (the buying public) will feel after they read the ad. The font they use, colors and adjectives, will directly influence whether you buy that product or even walk into the store. A very casual font will seem more inviting than a staunch, sharp letter. Look around at signs, see if they match the feeling of the store you are about to enter. Most pedestrian walkways, police signs and government postings, are done with the same font—Times Roman or Helvetica. Fancier ads and signs use a fancier font.

How does this correlate with the voice-over artist? It helps to understand the writer's intention when reading copy. This is just another level to explore that may help you interpret your read when you go in for the audition. If the copy is written like this:

> **SAVE $1.00 off your next purchase of**
> **TASTY CHICKEN TACO Supreme,**
> **the next time you come into TACO BELL.**
> **SAVOR the munchies!**

There are exceptions—often the copy of just plain typewriter style. As a general rule, when writers add these nuances, they are done for a reason. And you should read accordingly. There isn't a secret code that tells you how to emphasize a bold word, but the general feeling is that you should emphasize it more than the other words.

Most copy/scripts are typed out. Only when a writer has a rewrite (changing the original script) will it be handwritten.

Deep Breathing: Take Five, Relax and Inhale/Exhale

There are deep breathing exercises that you can do to relax, so you don't put so much energy into being nervous. Take a deep breath. Inhale through the nose, hold it for a few seconds and then exhale through the mouth, breathing it all out. Think calm thoughts. Relax. Do this ten or more times, and you will calm your mind and be able to concentrate on the work. You need to create relaxation in you're work, not nervous energy.

Now that we've incorporated a grasp of the language, interpretation of character, depth of emotion, phrasing of words and punctuation, it's time to add another technical aspect that will help make or break your technique.

TIMING OF DIALOGUE

The timing of the spot is important for a number of reasons. First of all, from the director, writer or client standpoint, the timing is the first thing they work on. Is it a 30 second radio spot? Is it a 60 second TV spot? How much time do we have to fit in what we want to say?

The writing of the spot along with the concept are the first things that the ad agency and client come up with. By the time the voice-over artist gets it, the copy's been through a number of changes and time constraints. The timing of a spot has to do with fitting in what the client wants the ad agency to say in the spot and how much air time they are planning to buy to run the spot. The client may say, "We want a 30 second spot for radio, but want to fit in this much dialogue, and make it fun and upbeat."

> "Today only, 30% off all kid's Dockers and women's sandals. Tomorrow until 5:00 p. m. get 2 for 1 on Nike socks, that's 2 for 1 tomorrow until 5:00 only at K-Mart. K-Mart, the place you love to shop."

The ad agency writer(s) will still have to create a fun, entertaining spot. They have to write dialogue around the information. That information is the last to be edited out of the read because the client wants this information in the copy. Part of the writer's job is to fit the information in, along with creating an interesting spot, while fitting all of this in the proper time allowed.

Timing tells you two things about a read:

It tells you how fast you should go. What is the pace of the script? If there is wall to wall dialogue (Meaning that the dialogue fills up the entire read, without any pauses or time for music and/ or sound effects before or after) you will need to read accordingly.

It tells you what the writer has intended by the length of the script. Does the writer want the read slow and casual or does the writer want you to be quick, high paced and energetic? Sometimes if a script is 30 seconds and you've done the read several times, you may not be able to get the read in 30. At that point, the writer will shorten/edit the script, taking out words that don't matter as much and aren't selling points (informative pieces of the product), so you will have more time with the copy and the writer will get more of the read that they want.

Timing is the basic essence of a spot. It tells you (the reader) how long you have to play around with certain words, phrases, sentences and the entire spot. You may also be working with another voice-over artist and you will be given different times to work with your dialogue. They may want to shorten your read or lengthen it, depending on what the writer is aiming for.

EMPHASIS, INFLECTION, ACCENTS AND SYLLABLES

When you are working with the director at a voice-over session, you will always get certain advice. You may read the copy with a particular inflection or word emphasis, and the director may have a completely different take on that read. Perhaps something you never even thought of. The director may stop you in the middle of a take and have you emphasize the read a completely different way. You may not even see the point of the direction, but the director and the clients are the boss! They have their reasons, so just go along with all changes.

Here's an example:

GET TO MERVYN'S SUPER SALE HOWEVER YOU CAN!

Through the work that you've done before you begin your read (interpretation of character, phrasing of words, emotion, who you are talking to) you may decided to emphasize certain words because they fit the mood or the description of what the director or writer said.

You may choose to emphasize "Mervyn's" and "However" just because that seems natural and fits rhythmically with your read. Or, you may emphasize them because that's the way the words came out when you were reading the copy. The director may ask you to emphasize "Get" and "Mervyn's" but throw away the rest. This is where different emphasis and inflection come in.

Now, let's be even more specific: Accents and syllables.

We generally put emphasis on certain letters or syllables because of how and where we were raised. Most people have some sort of accent—strong Southern, Australian, or New York accent— or an affectation of certain words or letters. The way in which someone elongates an E or I, the way in which they may cut off letters and syllables can identify where they are from. Everyone has a different way of speaking whether they are born in the midwest, the south, north, east or west. (After doing voice-overs for so many years, I can automatically tell when someone is from Philadelphia because of the way that they pronounce certain words and syllables.)

When you are doing voice-overs, you have to work on eliminating any noticeable accent. People with strong accents really don't book work (unless the script intentionally specifies a strong accent.) The accent, or dialect, will be included in the description. African-American, Indian, Venezuelan, Puerto Rican, French, etc., are all descriptions of accent styles.

If you think something would work with an Indian flair, go for it. I just don't know if you'll get the job. You may think, "Hey, this character would be funnier with a Spanish accent. " Do one version with your "American" accent and another with your "Spanish" accent. It could work. Don't do this for any it for television copy though. Television copy is very specific in their idea of what kind of voice they are looking for. Radio spots don't require any visuals, only sound effects and voice-over talent, so they are much less expensive and more open to improvisation.

What if I Have an Accent?

Depending on where you live (Georgia, for example), your accent may get you some local work. The way you speak will be familiar to people living in Atlanta.

If your accent is really strong, you will need to take some dialogue classes or go to a dialect coach to tone it down or eliminate it. There are books you can read that teach you proper enunciation. Also, learn how to pronounce words properly. The advertising world likes voice-over artists to be literate and have very little discernible accent.

Accents are used as descriptions, like I said above. This means that you *can* use your accent to your benefit at the appropriate time when that type of job comes up. You will have much more freedom with your accent in animation work. You can integrate the accent into your character even if the character isn't written to sound like a New Yorker or Valley Girl.

People say certain syllables differently. As long as you enunciate and don't run your words together, you are safe. Make sure that your mouth isn't dry and that you pronounce letters correctly. Try this tongue twister for a warm up:

How now brown cow

Slipping slowly into sloth

Wendy whines whenever William wonders where Wendy is.

You'll notice when you read copy, certain words are harder to say. An S next to an F may be difficult. To work on your enunciation skills, say the alphabet aloud, enunciating each letter fully.

Sometimes we speak so quickly that we drop letters. In voice-overs, the letters and words are all you've got, so you can't drop them. You can't say "ya" for "you," unless the director tells you it's okay. You can't say "Yeah" for "Yes." Everything is written for a reason. In that sense, even if you have a very casual informal session, it will still be considered formal in dialogue. You just won't be reading it that way. Your job as the voice-over actor is to take the more boring or formal copy and "give it life. "

Diction

Whether or not you use good diction depends upon what you are asked to do as a voice-over artist. I once created a character who had sloppy speech patterns and it worked for that job. Making sure that the name of the product comes out clearly is very important. If you can make sure your dialogue sounds crisp as well as conversational, you will have a good combination.

Pace

The pace, or speed at which you read the copy, depends on how the writer wrote the spot, and how the director wants it read. Find a comfortable pace that fits with the timing they prefer. Pacing also will fit with the rhythm of the spot. After reading the spot a few times, you will find that there is a natural rhythm. Once you find it, you should be able to read it in the time allotted.

There are many different ways that a spot can be read. Find the different ways. Find the pacing that feels right. We hear the words "real" a lot. Advertisers want a real, conversational read. So breathe naturally and read like you are talking to someone. The read and pacing will come naturally. Now, obviously you won't go into every read this way, but if you start from real, you will be a lot better off. Pretend you're talking to someone. Now tell them the story. The rhythm will come naturally.

Tone

Every voice-over spot, animated spot, promo, narration or promo has a tone—the general feeling of the sponser: serious, business, comedic, conversational, dry, thoughtful. Once you read the spot and get the feel of it, the written tone will help you decide what kind of inflection to use in your voice.

There are many different forms of tone: the feeling of the spot; the sound of the headphones (loud, soft); how your personality comes across in your read; how your actual voice sounds (high- or low-pitched). The pitch of your relates to your emotional state. Excited voices tend to go up to a higher pitch. If you are feeling introspective or intimate, your tone will be lower. You can learn to play with your tone of voice to convey different feelings and attitudes. (How many of us can remember hearing our mothers say, "Don't you take that tone with me!" It wasn't what we were saying, it was the bratty tone we used to say it!)

The tone of your read can be affected by where you stand in front of the microphone. If you are very close, almost touching the mike, your tone will be softer, quieter and more intimate. If you are standing far away, yelling from the sidelines or needing to be louder, your tone will be louder, more energetic and at a much higher level, vocally. How the headphone level is set will also affect what kind of tone you will give in the read.

Keep your tone of voice a the same level throughout your read, unless it is appropriate to change it. The copy or directions will indicate that.

When the sound engineer has asked for the "level," speak a few words from the copy using the same tone of voice that you will use when you read; the same loudness or softness, and the same relationship to the microphone. Teaching yourself where to stand, what is comfortable, will all come more naturally as you learn to work with the microphone. Soon, the awkwardness that you first feel will disappear and this will all be second nature to you. The booth that seems so small and cramped will feel cozy.

If you are trying for an intimate read, keep your level consistent. Don't suddenly get louder and then softer. The read should reflect the attitude of the spot. Your voice is the direct correlation between the mood of what the writer is trying to convey.

☞ *Keep the same distance from the mike during your entire read.*

TONE VS. ATTITUDE

Tone and attitude are very different. Tone is your vocal quality and general vocal feeling of the spot, whereas the attitude is the emotion you are feeling while conveying it. The attitude will affect the tone.

Tone vs. Pitch

Tone and pitch, are two different things. Your pitch is the level of your vocal quality. The tone is affected by the pitch. You can read with one tone and then pick several different pitches within your voice. You can be speaking very soft and low, but still change your vocal pitch from very low pitched to high pitched, never changing the tone of the spot.

Hazards

Popping those P's, spitting, losing your breath, coughing, choking, body parts falling asleep (arms, hands, toes) itchy tongue, sneezing and any other hazard you can think of can and will happen to anyone, even the most seasoned professionals, at one time or another.

You cannot expect to read perfectly every time. Something will get caught in your throat, you won't be able to swallow, you'll feel a sneeze coming on, you'll be in the middle of a read and a P will pop out and hit the microphone and reverberate into the studio. What do you do?

Relax. There is nothing you can do, except realize these are all normal functions; even popping P's is normal. If you have a tendency to pop your P's or slur certain words, the sound engineer, after hearing you read, will put a filter on the microphone. This will protect your read so that every little squeak, squabble and pop won't shoot out and be so easy to detect. What about detectable breathing? In any voice-over you listen to, if you listen hard enough, you will be able to hear breathing. That is because you cannot read a spot without breathing. Make sure that you give yourself enough time between sentences and before sentences to get through the sentence without taking another deep breath.

Voice-over artists have strong vocal control just like singers, yet we don't hold on notes or practice by singing the lines. After you've read for a long time, you will be able to control your breathing.

As an exercise, read this sentence and see if you can say the whole line in one breath. You probably can't. Or, if you did, it sounded hurried and unnatural. Now, during the period, breathe in, and then finish the sentence until you've said the entire thought in two breaths.

See how far you can get in the sentence before you have to take a breath. Count the breaths and try again. Work on getting through that sentence in two breaths without sounding short of breath. Try this with the sample copy in Appendix A. You will find the natural places to breathe in the way that the dialogue is written. Give yourself a test. Even if you can breathe every period in a spot, go longer. Try to build up your resistance and get the entire thought in one breath without making it sound like you're struggling.

Smokers have shorter breathing ability. Swimmers have longer. Swimmers are exercising their lungs as well as anyone that does cardio-vascular exercise at least 25 minutes a day. Your breathing ability will improve with more cardio-vascular exercise.

What's Next?

Now that you've learned the basics to your icing (your voice) relax, take that deep breath, and put the information in the back of your head. Now let the creative part of you come forward. This is the most important part of your read. The technical part is for adjustments and tweaking. Now that you have that knowledge, you need to solely rely on your God-given talent to read that spot!

> *I treat every audition as just that: an audition. I go in, study the copy, incorporate my ideas, find the character, give the best read I can for how I see the character and copy. Then I leave. I don't worry about how I read something. If I book the job, then I book the job. I can't worry about what I did right or wrong. If I go in with the attitude that I don't NEED something, then I am free to do good work, no matter if they want me or not, and this leaves me free to experiment.*

Technique is whatever you make it. My technique is that I get out of my own way, so that I am there for the copy. I do a certain style of read that I got known for, which is a flat, sarcastic type of read, but whatever attitude they call for is what you should be available to do. Just make sure that you are coming from something, a story, an idea, a person in mind, a character, a feeling, a mood, a topic, a range, an emotion.

And then remember: JUST BREATHE.

Once you have practiced for awhile, this comes naturally. Don't worry about all the technical aspects of stance, microphone, breathing, popping your P's. Classes will help and being on the microphone will help. Remember just take ten deep breaths and relax. Now you can get out of your own way and have some fun.

An Interview with . . .
CHRIS ZIMMERMAN,
Animation Director and Casting Director

Chris Zimmerman is a very successful casting director and director of many animated shows. Her resume includes; *Cow & Chicken, I. M. Weasel, Book Of Virtues, B.R.U.N.O. The Kid, Mortal Kombat, Jonny Quest, G. I. Joe, Captain Planet, Dumb And Dumber, Swat Kats*, and many more. She also directs and casts animated episodes, CD-ROMs, Prime Tape, including *The Blues Brothers, Fish Police*; live action, M.O.W.'s and PSA's (just to name a few; her resume is very extensive)

What do you look for in a voice?
Everything from a rasp, speech pattern, attitude, all that can help identify a character. A lot of times it's the delivery rather than the actual voice qualities. When you audition, you'll get to read a paragraph or two, or a scene, with another actor. What nails the job is when the actor finds something to bring it the character to life.

Work the script your own. Use your oddity in speech pattern. The person who gets the job is the one who sometimes breaks the rules, who doesn't read the script the same way. The person who hones out the life of the character will get the job. Live the script, be present as the character in the present.

What about improvising?
Be aware of who you audition for. Improvising can be helpful to you, it makes you seem funnier. Don't overdo or you will kill your audition. Use it for the character. Don't show off. I don't mind improvising if it is appropriate to the scene and to the character.

What will help a voice-actor get re-hired after the voice session with you?
Show me your creative spark as an actor. Listen to the director. Hear what I ask for and respond. Attitude is a big requirement. I want actors to act, play, bring life to the room. You also need to be pleasant and easy to work with. The people who are willing to give 100 percent while they are there, will definitely be back.

How do you feel about getting unsolicited animation tapes?
If a tape looks professional or is from a union member I will accept

it. I try to listen to as many as I can. You need a tape to get in the door. I've never hired directly from demo tape. But, I have called people in from the demo tape. The voice-over tape is the calling card.

What makes a voice-over actor "good" in your book?
They become the character.

What advice would you give to new talent or talent who hasn't booked a lot of animation?
Get as much experience as you can in front of microphone. Actual jobs, auditions or workshops. Be comfortable in front of the microphone. You can't watch yourself; you can't be afraid to make a fool out of yourself.

Do you hire a lot of celebrities for voice-over jobs?
Yes, but I prefer to hire the person who is right for the part.

How closely do you work with the animators?
Some animators will come to the session to watch the actors. In feature work, the session is video taped so they can match the facial expression with the animation.

Any final word of advice?
Just free yourselves up to live the character. Free yourselves up as actors and BE FUN!

• • •

CHAPTER 4

ANIMATION, LOOPING, DUBBING, CD-ROMS, AUDIO BOOKS AND PROMOS

• • •

There many ways of making money in voice-overs. We've talked about commercials, which seems to be the most obvious area. However, many people make a healthy living in other areas of voice-overs that we will discuss in this chapter. Don't get too cocky yet; just because you work a lot in one area, doesn't mean that you will work in all them. Some voice-over artists who work in "looping" (re-recording dialogue that was missed or didn't record properly when originally taped or filmed) can't break into animation, or promos. Just focus on one thing and eventually you may get the opportunity to work in other areas.

> *I started doing regular commercials and wanted to break into promos. Interestingly enough, just as I wanted to start doing them, my agent started getting calls for me to come audition for some at the studios. I started booking. Now, I divide my time between commercial voice-overs and promos. A friend who does a lot of animation work also works part-time in a "loop group." Using our talents in multiple areas gives us more chance to make money in different areas.*

Looping, ADR (Audio Dialogue Replacement), Walla

Working in these categories requires no particular type of voice but plenty of acting skills. When looping, you will be required to follow a story that you see on screen and integrate your voice ability to the picture. "Loop groups" use experienced actors who can create reality to any given scene they are watching. They may require accents if it fits a scene they are looping.

Breaking into looping is not easy. You will need to join a "loop group." Having someone in a loop group refer you is the best way to break in. But don't forget to send your tape, as well, even if you don't know anyone. Acting experience is necessary. Previous experience in voice-overs helps. You may be hired to walla an entire medical emergency/hospital scene that has twenty or more actors walking through the scene. The loop group will have to re-create that entire scene through voice dialogue. Although the camera will be pulled back enough that you cannot see who is saying what, you still get the illusion that each character and background actor who walks through the scene is actually saying the words. Everyone from an ER nurse over the intercom to the patient on a gurney. You will be required to come up with phrases and dialogue to match what is going on in the scene. *There will be no script.* Improvisational skills are highly important in looping. Your ability to watch a scene once and come up with dialogue fitting for that scene is extremely important. You may have several group scenes and you may be required to do a written weather and/or news report that needs to be looped. This is something that you will have to write down and then act out in the scene when you see it appear on the large screen before you.

If you are part of a loop group, you need to be able to work well with a group. They call it being part of a vocal orchestra. You need to know when to be loud, soft, angry, nice, sad, happy. You will duplicate the exact mood of what's on the screen. It's important to always face the microphone even though you may be several feet away to allow room to move around and stand in a crowd with other people. Several loopers may stand around you, in front of many microphones, looping the same scene at the same time. You have to know, in certain scenes, how to change dialogue rapidly as you see the scene unfold in front of you.

In the scene you are going to loop, a policeman may walk from his car, tell onlookers to stand back, walk into a house, setting off an alarm as a dog runs out. The loopers are responsible for all the background dialogue and action. This means they have to cover every background actor, including talk coming from a police dispatch as the policeman closes his car, to the dog running out, barking. This is a lot of hard work. The loopers may do this several times until the scene sounds real. Your job as the looper is to re-create the scene exactly as it would be happening if it were a real scenario. In the original movie or television show, the extras will just have watched, not saying anything. The director knows that the voices and ambiance will be covered during the editing period (post production.) The production company will hire a loop group to fill in the noise.

Depending on where you stand while looping and if you are wearing headphones, can create the illusion of being indoors and outdoors. Standing farther away without headphones gives the illusion of being outside. Several loopers, standing several inches from the microphones, yelling to the sides and away from directly to the microphone, will sound like they're outside. Just the opposite is true for a more intimate one on one read. Headphones and standing right up to the microphone, gives the illusion of being inside and even standing intimately next to one another at a party, telling a secret.

To find loop groups in your town, call production companies or ask your agent or union. You can join as many loop groups as will take you. Most loopers know each other because it's such a small market of actors. Loop groups are union. Your pay scale will be according to what you decide with the looping company or film you are looping. You can ask your agent to help get you in with a loop group, but it will take away from your other auditions because loopers can work all day. An agent would rather book you on regular commercials or animation because the pay is better and there is a chance for more work. Looping is a rather long job compared to commercials. With a television or radio spot, you may only be in a session for an hour, but with looping it can be as long as eight-hour days. You have to be able to commit to a project, once they hire you. Most loopers either know someone to help get them in that are already in the business or will send their commercial demo tape to the loop groups. Take a class on looping so you will know what it entails.

LOOPING DO'S AND DON'TS
(courtesy of Sandy Holt's Loop Ease)

- DO come to the session prepared. Know material you are looping. Know which genre the material belongs to. (e. g., drama, comedy, science-fiction)
- DO know your jargon: military, scientific, period piece, medical, police, fire, action.
- DO be a team player. Accommodate other actors and your sound engineer or whomever is running the session.
- DO take direction well!

- DO follow what is going on in the story!
- DO pay attention to each scene on the screen even if your not looping that particular scene. You need to know what's going on from each scene to the next.
- DO empty keys and change from pockets, remove jewelry, anything that makes a noise.

- DON'T talk during playback of what you've just recorded.
- DON'T talk during a take unless your supposed to during the scene.
- DON'T purposely drown out other actors unless it's within the scene and your supposed to be louder.
- DON'T ever use proper names of products such as Sony, Coke, Nike, Reebok,Tide. Use generic terms.
- DON'T overpower other actors. Keep voice quality and dialogue appropriate for scene to match other actors in the scene.
- DON'T use negative tones or dialogue during walla. (Unless the scene calls for it.)

DUBBING

Dubbing requires you to match a voice. Your sole job is to copy and match the original actor's tone and voice quality. Most dubbing is from one language to another (e. g., French to English, Spanish to English.) You may need to know the original language so that you will know when to follow along on the dialogue. Vocal sound and texture depends on whose voice you are dubbing. Timing is also very important. You will need to match voice to picture.

This work can be found through Post Production facilities and through your union. Call for details. This work is both union and nonunion. They also use a lot of the same people over and over again once you're in.

From time to time, voice-over actors may be called in to "dub" an actual line of dialogue in an English-language film. If an actor, who has only a single line, is shown on camera so that you never see their face, the director may hire a voice-over actor to say the line instead of calling back the original actor. This happens for many reasons: 1) the director may have not liked the placement of the actual line and wants it to be spoken earlier or later; 2) the director may have not liked the person's voice; 3) the actor wasn't available to do the dub. In any case, a looper will be chosen to dub that line(s). The voice-over actor will try to match in voice quality to the other person or match what they think that person would sound like. A really mousy sounding girl's voice spoken by a Cindy Crawford-type actor won't work. Voices need to match.

ANIMATION

Animation is creating different characters for the enormous and ever-increasing animation market. Animation was once was relegated to "Saturday morning cartoons." Now you will find animation on CD ROM's, multimedia presentations, films, television shows, prime time and, of course, still on Saturday mornings.

To be successful in animation requires an acting background as well as an interesting voice. There isn't one type of voice in animation; the important aspect is that your voice is unique or that you can do unique things with it. The best way to enter the animation field is to take a class. Start putting all of those weird voices that you've done for years at home, to work for you.

Animation work is lucrative and tight to get in. You are better off with animation in the larger cities, although you never know if there may be some local animation festival or cartoon show or commercial. Animation work is mostly union work.

NARRATION

The narrator is a person telling a story, and these people also get paid for their voice work. Narrators are on television, radio, industrial films (non-commercial films for a particular industry), infomercials, documentaries and theatrical films. Narrator's voices are usually well-modulated, soothing or deep.

Small industrial films and in-house video work may be the easiest work to get in the smaller towns, or if you're non-union. Local television and radio shows, fashion shows, in house promotional store sales, projects with ad agencies all need narrators. Post Production houses also may hire a narrator for a project once it is in the finishing stages.

The in-house or industrial film is for non-broadcast, meaning that it will not be aired. It is used solely for the company that hired you to do the work. It is to show employees or future clients their product. You are hired to do the voice-over that tells about whatever the product or procedure that they are showing to the client or employees. This work can be union and non-union.

CD-ROM/DVD/Laserdisc

A CD-ROM is a computer disk that uses voices to accent the music, narrate a story, or act in an animated series or film. They can be educational or entertaining. The voice-over artist can tell a story as the picture is being played or be one of the characters. You can view the disk on your computer, or on your television (Laser Disk, DVD).

The multimedia field presents great opportunities for voice-over actors, as all types of talent are needed. Most CD-ROM work is non-union for now. The unions are just working on making it union and figuring out what to charge. Meantime, the companies are hiring the agencies on a daily basis, the agent or you need to come up with a price. The hours can be long and the work is tedious, but there will be a great mass of work in the near future. If you are non-union, this is a good area to try to go into. Check production facilities, advertising agencies, and local yellow pages.

Books on Tape/Audio Books

"Books on Tape" or audio books are voice-overs of books. Children's stories as *Peter Pan*, *Winnie The Pooh*, *Hansel and Gretel* probably come to mind first, but this huge market includes fiction, non-fiction, how-tos, best-sellers, classic literature, and more. If you are good at reading aloud, then you should have success in this market, as that is what you will be doing on tape: reading from a book. Audio books can use all sorts of voices, depending on the subject matter.

There are companies across the U.S. that specialize in this. In the appendix are listed some companies in the Los Angeles area. To find others, you will need to do some research. Look in your local bookstores for the names of audio book companies and contact them. Or, if you have access to the Internet, do an online search for audio books.

Once you have a list of companies and names, send each person a demo tape. The work is long and the hours are long, but the pay can be good. The work is both union and non-union depending on the company and the job.

Promotional Spots (Promos)

Promos are the essence of an entire commercial whittled down to a single thought. Promos are also those short announcements you hear at the end of one show announcing the name, date, time and most important information that you need to know about another program, film, documentary or ad. (See promo sample copy in Appendix A.)

Men used to dominate the world of promos. That has changed somewhat due to channels such as Lifetime that air more female-oriented programs. Women's voices are being heard more frequently. Promo voices tend to be more authoritative, even deeper in tone. Watch television to get a feel for what promo voices sound like. They will tend to match the show they are pitching. Light and breezier for *Mad About You,* more serious for *Dateline.* Lifetime uses very smooth, deep, warm women's voices, where UPN Sport Network goes for a more manly, throaty quality. How about news programs? They use more of a conservative, authoritative voice. Think Dan Rather.

The promo world is exciting. You could go from doing the promos for a television or radio station in your home town, to doing national promos in Los Angeles or New York. The work is steady and it pays well. They use the same people over and over again. These are union jobs unless you are doing the work in a smaller city for a local TV or radio station.

Trailers/Teasers

Trailers ("teasers") are mini-commercials for a television show or film. They tell you everything you need to know about a full length feature in less than a minute. If done well, the trailer will sell you the story, before you've had a chance to see the product. They are designed to pull you into the product they are selling so that you will want to see the whole thing. Voice-overs for trailers are mostly done by men, although a few women are starting to do them as well.

Do some research and find out which companies producer trailers. These are the companies who hire the vocal talent. Send them a tape and don't give up.

Can I Make Money In Any of These Fields?

Of course. Listen to all those voices you hear. Who do you think is doing them? The work is out there. Pick a field of study and follow that road to achieving it. It's rare that you would succeed in all aspects of the voice-over business, it's too vast. But if you pick one or two areas and concentrate, there's no telling what you can do!

An Interview with . . .
DEBBY DERRYBERRY, Animation Voice-over Actress

First, let's get your resume out of the way. What shows are you on or have you recently done?
I'm Judy on *Jumanji*; on *Bobby's World*, I'm Bobby's girlfriend; *Life With Louie*, Jeanie; and a new show that I hoping will be picked up, *Bad Baby*. I also did *Tazmanian Devil* and was Tinkerbell in *Peter Pan and the Pirates*.

Wow, quite a list! How did you get started?
I was living in Nashville doing child jingles. I sent my demo tape to Los Angeles. Ginny McSwain, an animation Casting Director, responded back to me because she liked the tape. She told me that I would have to move to Los Angeles to get work. When I moved out here, I re-submitted all of my tapes again. Ginny set me up a meeting with an agent and he signed me. That was nine years ago.

How do you create the voices that you do?
By the picture. I try to look at the picture if they have one or the character description. If the character is nerdy, I try to stand the way that I think the character would, do the physical aspect of the character. I try to emulate the character. It helps to create the attitude of the character. The attitude is much more important in getting the job than "tweaking" it a certain way.

What's your signature voice?
I'm the little girl. Either the bratty girl, or the uppercrust snobby girl, the sweet angel girl. It depends on who is casting. Each casting director may see you in a different way.

What was your first job and how long did it take you to book it?
I booked my first job after my third audition. It was a special on TV called *Dixie's Diner*. I was a southern bell pig. Then I booked *Tiny Tunes*. My next job was *Peter Pan and the Pirates* with Tim Curry. They signed us to 65 episodes. I was Tinkerbell's first voice.

Sixty-five episodes is what we all want to get. Are most of your animated series for 65 episodes?
Usually, they don't sign you for that many. That is rare. A show may go for that many episodes, but most likely unless you're a

celebrity, you will be paid per episode, no matter how many you do. They will pay you for the pilot, then thirteen, then if you're lucky and the show goes to 65! Disney pays residuals for ten re-runs, right up front. Most shows pay you for residuals, each time it plays. We all work for scale, day-player rate.

Any other characters that you specialize in?
Interestingly enough, I get a lot of work doing "Infant cries." There is a big call for it, and I'm their girl. I looped an animation feature with infant cries.

Do you do a lot of looping?
Yes. I do animation, looping and regular voice-over commercials.

Which do you prefer between looping and animation?
I enjoy both. An animation day is shorter. You will work on a TV show for four hours and a looping session for eight. An animation day is shorter for better money.

What about residuals on animation features?
You get the residuals when it goes to video. The big money is in video sales. I giggled in *TOY STORY* and the money has been great. Animated Disney makes you a lot of money. On TV, you get the residuals when they re-run the show.

Do you still have to audition for a part on an animated show?
For principal roles I do. For special guests spots, they usually just call me in. I started out doing a special guest for *Casper* and they liked what I did, so it turned into a regular role.

How do you stand out in animation? Is their room for improvisation?
Absolutely! It's what makes your character stand out! If you can get away with improvising, then go for it! Incorporate it into the character. You still have a certain time frame that you have to stick to, but there is room to play within the read. Improvising is what can make you stand out from being a special guest to a regular role. There is always room for padding.

Can you give me an example of an improvised moment?
Sure. On *Bobby's World*, there was a line that said "Ouch, I hurt my knee." I changed it to, "Bobby, I have an abrasion."

What did the director do?
They loved it. In fact, they sometimes have the animators come to the voice-over session to meet you and watch what you do while you're recording. They want to see how you are reading the copy. While you are reading the copy, what your physical body is doing; How you're holding your arms, squishing your face to get that certain sound or attitude. I've watched the cartoon at a later date and seen that my character is doing the same physical act that I did in the session. I've seen *Tinkerbell* cross her eyes, in a scene where I had crossed my eyes saying the line in the session. The animators saw it and loved it, so they incorporated it into the character!

That's great! Do you have any "ritual" that you go through for your voice?
I read the script. Highlight my lines. I do all my improvisation the night before the audition. Be ready! I read the verbal cues in the script. Running, jumping, out of breathe, throwing a ball. You have to know when to incorporate a "hmph," or heavy breathing within the sentence. If your character is falling, know when to get louder, to yell, to get softer. To make it seem like you are really doing these things. The description of the character helps tells you what to do and what the character is like.

How many characters do you think that you have inside of you?
Off the top, I would say about twelve. Within those twelve, I have about ten different dialects for each character.

Which dialects?
Oh, I can do Texas, Georgia, New York, England, Ireland, Valley girl, Russian, Norwegian and a bunch more.

How do you create new characters?
You find them within the pictures, The auditions. The copy. What the character says, how they act, how they look. Sometimes if it seems that they would have a lisp, or braces, or glasses. All in the style of the character.

Do you have any advice to new talent trying to break into animation?
Remain humble. Be persistent. Get your tape out. Re-submit every six months. Keep taking classes with casting directors. It is very important to know every casting director in town. I still bring my

tape to auditions. I just dropped it off for a certain audition and they happened to like something on there, so they hired me for another role as special guest, not the audition that I originally read for. So, it's always good to have your tape to show your range.

How tough is it to break in?
Extremely tough. It's very competitive. The casting directors have their favorites. I would spend all of my money on meeting the casting directors. Go to classes!

What's a normal week/day like for you?
Well, If I'm on a series, we work once a week. A normal schedule for a show would be Tuesday, 2 to 6. Otherwise, I may loop 9 to 6 and during lunch, run across town for an audition. Or I may do a voice-over session from 10-2, grab some lunch and run around to several auditions all over town.

An Interview with . . .
Frank Muller, Audio Book Narrator

Frank Muller is one of the most highly-regarded narrators of audio books. His reputation is tops.

I refer to audio books as "books on tape." Is that the correct term?
Books On Tape is actually a company based in Newport Beach, California. They were one of the first companies to come up with the idea of audio books and they patented the name. The correct name is "audio books," the generic term for the medium that covers the recording of any and all printed matter.

How did you get started in the audio books business?
A traveling salesman started a business recording books and came in to the regional theatre where I was working. He was looking for actors to record books on audio tape. He started the business because he wanted to be able to listen to books while traveling in his car.

What was your first job?
It was 1979, and the book was *The Seawolf* by Jack London. Then I did *Call of the Wild.*

How long does it take to record a book?
It depends. Typically, you are in a studio three to four hours for 25 to 35 pages, depending on the density of the pages. A 300-page book generally will take around nine to ten hours. It depends on whether you are recording an abridged or unabridged book.

Can you clarify?
In the mid '80s, all the publishing houses jumped in and wanted to do the audio books. They thought that they would make a fortune. But the publishing houses didn't want to record the complete, or unabridged, versions of the books. So, they hired editors to "abridge" or shorten the book so that the it would fit onto a two-hour tape.

Many people prefer the unabridged versions. They don't like losing the character and ambiance that you do with abridged versions.

They want to feel they are getting the same thing as if they picked up the book and read it themselves. Classics are usually recorded as unabridged works.

Do publishing houses prefer abridged or unabridged versions?
In the past, after the publishing houses got involved, they only wanted to do abridged. They felt they would sell better. Major publishing houses such as Penguin and Warner, are now dabbling in unabridged. And there are some companies that just sell unabridged.

How much do unabridged audio books sell for?
A John Grisham or Stephen King novel would sell for around $30 to $40. This is for a 14- to 16-hour audio book.

How do you record that much time and not hurt your voice?
I'm used to doing it. But it's a full-time job. I work seven to eight hours a day. I just bring some hot tea or water into the room.

Do you record at a recording studio like other voice talent?
Yes. However, I've been doing them for so long that I built a studio in my house. The publishing companies call me directly. Most other narrators go to a studio and work with a producer just like a regular session.

How are audio books cast?
Many people work through their agent, just like booking regular commercials. Most people, though, only do two to four books a year. Right now, there really isn't a good contract through AFTRA. And the work is longer hours and much tougher than regular commercial work. When casting, they tend to cast one person to read the book . . . the entire book.

Does more than one person do the narration on any individual audio book?
Usually one voice-over person (narrator) will do the entire read. The single voice recording preserves the intimacy of the recording and the experience of the novel. You alone will play the different voices. It is a lot of acting work. You need to be able to be very animated and come up with several different voices all fitting the characters as you are telling the story.

Can different publishing companies sell different versions of the story?
It's a very competitive business. There can be many different versions of the same book depending on the deal that the publishing house has signed. If they have signed a non-exclusive deal, than other publishing companies can do their version of the audio book.

For a fee, an independent audio company will get to record the book.

The publishing company will control the audio publisher's rights. The publishing house may also sell their rights to independents who will do a version of the book, abridged or unabridged. There may be several different abridged or unabridged version of the same book. Each one will have been narrated by someone different, each version of the book, slightly different. Each company will use their own "abridger."

Are there any books that you did and know that someone else also read?
Pat Conroy, who wrote *Prince of Tides*, also wrote *Beach Music*. I did an unabridged version that was 27 hours long. There were three different versions of that book. The abridged version is nine hours long.

How do you analyze the dialogue and story when reading the audio book?
Cormac McCarthy, who wrote *All the Pretty Horses,* (Matt Damon is starring in the movie version) doesn't use quotation marks when he writes. I have to guess at the conversation when reading the dialogue.

What have you been working on?
I just finished *On the Road* by Jack Kerouac. We did an exclusive, which means that no other audio book can be done. It was great to do!

I'll bet. What else?
Just did a Larry McMurtry book. 24 hours. It took all summer.

That's a lot of work. How about dialect?
I do tons of research for each book. I break down the script beforehand, but I don't make all of my choices before. I keep a bank of dictionaries handy: medical, foreign language, veterinary, geographical and biographical. It's a big acting challenge. You have to develop characterizations.

What kind of fee does a narrator get for a book?
If you are a top dog, you work as a buy-out. There is no set fee per book. Some companies do have waiver agreements. Most people

work non-union and negotiate a fee with the company they are working with. Technically, AFTRA is the union and it falls under narration, but they don't really know what area to put it under. The union hasn't organized that part of the industry yet. Usually, you are paid a flat rate per book. But this is clearly individual. Whatever you negotiate with the company is what you get.

What do you teach in your class?
I give you tools, including direction, to learn the dynamics of getting into and playing the scene. Creating the setting for the listener.

How about if we end with a quote about audio books. Got one?
"It's a re-incarnation of the ancient art of storytelling."

CHAPTER 5

• • •
INTERPRETING THE READ
• • •

> *I was known for business straight reads, and then high energy reads until the HomeBase campaign came along. Then all the sudden I was the stereotype for the flat read. I didn't set out to do that. It just happened. I created different types of reads for each type of product according to what the advertiser was looking for. Sometimes that is the best way to find the different types of reads to add to your imaginary "rolodex of voices."*

Let's start with the piece of copy (the script) that you will need to analyze and interpret in a certain way.

Ask yourself the following questions:

- What time should I read the copy in? (This will be somewhere on the copy)
- How will I know what "character" to use? (Usually a character description will be on the bottom of the copy)
- How should I interpret what the advertiser is trying to say? (Use the description and the type of copy what kind of read they are looking for)
- Where do I begin? (Study the copy, think about what the advertiser is selling and the audience they want to reach.)

HELP!

"Help!" may be your only choice, you feel. But really, the work is simple.

Don't get ahead of what you know!

Don't be a mind reader!

Do not assume you know how to sell the product better than the advertiser!

What you DO know is what the product is!

It's important to see what you are selling. If there is no picture and it's radio copy, know what they are selling and what they are trying to say. You may not be always be given the luxury of direction. You can tell a lot by the copy, by what it says, what the product is and all the other clues we've discussed throughout the book. Remember to look at the font and writing style. If you have a picture to go by (television or animation), this helps in determining character. (See sample copy in Appendix A.)

Most of the time, the ad agency will supply some sort of direction on the copy. If not, you can always ask the casting director (or your agent if you are at your agency). The directions, or the jargon in which they are written, may still be confusing to you. Some of the ins and outs of this business will take some time to learn. This book is meant to help you, show you some of the copy, direct you on your path in the voice-over world so that it won't seem so strange.

DIRECTION

The direction does not, however, give you the answer to the puzzle of how to read the spot perfectly. It just helps fill in a few blanks. Use the direction as a guide. There are still hundreds of different kinds of reads you can give. But if you do not have any direction to follow (this does happen) then you need to follow your instinct or gut feeling.

Read the copy. Use your knowledge. Let's run through this copy for cat food below and analyze it.

"Violet Variety Cat food. Make your cat purr for life!"

Now, decide what type of spot this is. Remember, "type of spot" means the style of spot or type of read. This will be easier to identify the more copy and commercials that you read. Identifying styles and types of spots will come from reading the dialogue and understanding what the ad agency is trying to sell and how.

This can be difficult if you are just provided the product name, but from the name alone, here's what I can decipher:

Some types of spots this ad could be:

SOFT SELL

SEXY SELL

INTIMATE SELL

PLAYFUL SELL

See how many reads that we came up with just with the name of the product?! This is the same process you will go through with every commercial that you read for. This applies to animation as well. You will have the copy and/or a picture with a description. You will have to decide what kind of character will go with what you are seeing and reading.

Let's go back for a moment to "Violet Variety Cat Food." Read the product name and tag line three times each differently for each one of the four types of reads.

Now try another three, putting two or more of the sells together. Change the level of your voice. Try a sexy sell three times changing octaves as you read each one. Make one sexy sell, louder. Make another sexy sell fun. Make your third sexy sell, more intimate and commanding.

See how each time you read it, you get a different feel for the spot?

Take a few minutes, grab your recorder and look through the sample copy in Appendix A. Pick one or two spots. Spend some time looking at the direction and deciding what kind of sell would be most effective.

Okay, let's move further. Here is some sample copy:

"Sam is a sports fanatic. I can't call him during the day, because some sport is on, I can't call him at night, because. . . well you got it, so when do I call him? He never answers the phone. Especially since he got the call check from AT&T. Now all he's got to do is look at the little number that shows up on the box, which he keeps on the floor, next to his LazyBoy chair, next to the pretzels, next to the beer. This way, when he's looking for the box, it'll be where he doesn't have to go very far. So you think Sam is ever on the phone? Only if it's Sadie with a beer run call! And he knows her car number by heart. What a guy!"

The casting director and the script will tell you whether the copy is for television or radio. You also will be able to tell because of the way that it is typed. Television commercial copy has two columns: the left describes the visual, and the right shows the actual words to be said. Read only from the right hand side.

The radio copy usually will just have the length of spot at the top and the copy typed any number of ways. Radio copy is usually pretty obvious to spot. Radio spots make up for the lack of pictures by having more words. Sometimes, you will find even fewer words depending on what is being sold. For example, AirTouch Cellualr has used the silence in the conversation between two voice-over artists in their radio spots to convey the clarity of their service.

Read the AT&T copy three different ways. Record it and listen back.

There are many different ways to interpret this copy. They could want a man or a woman. Young or old. Sarcastic or empathetic. This read could be done very straight and objective by an older gentleman with very little humor as if they were selling strictly from the store, or it could be hip, young, fun and dry.

It could also be read by a woman, late '40s, acting as if she were talking with a neighbor about the fact that Sadie is working for her husband., Or it could just a be Sam's buddy trying to get in touch with him. Regular guy, sense of wryness, off the wall, simple and direct. There are so many different types of reads.

If I were reading this copy without direction, my first instinct would be to read this off the cuff (not too much force with the words) fun, relaxed, and dry. In my second take, I may do a more biting read with higher energy, and then I may do it straighter with just a hint of humor in certain places.

PLAY WITH THE READ! Find ten different ways to read this copy. Record it and listen back. You will be surprised at the reads you find.

The above copy is instinctively funny and sardonic. You know that just by what they are saying. But within the humor, there are still so many ways to approach the copy and still get different reads.

When doing radio spots, all you are selling is your voice saying the words. With TV, you have the luxury of a picture and a lot more space than with radio. A television commercial can be as simple as a picture of a dog being pet by an owner with a tag line saying:

Yours for life. Purina

You already get a feeling from the visual in the commercial. What kind of read would you do for the Purina spot? Do you think you should be high energy? Should you be intimate, laid back? Should a teenage boy read this copy? An older woman? A man?

Let's try another bit of copy:

"There were 134,000 smoking deaths last year. Should I reserve a space for you? This message has been brought to you by the California Anti-Smoking Department of Greater Health."

This, obviously, is a serious-straight, informative ad. We can interpret that by what the copy says. It is trying to reach us with assertiveness, knowledge and a little touch of sarcasm. The way that you read the copy should reflect the same.

Try to read the copy five different ways. Attempt this with strength, knowledge, slight humor, anger, warmth, empathy, relaxed, straight read, simple, sexy, with an edge. Just giving you some examples of the way that this copy could be interpreted.

Read aloud. Record. Listen back. See what you come up with.

Push and Pull Back

How do you know which words or phrases to push? Or which ones to pull back on?

"Push" is a term used in voice-overs when we want to stress certain words. Other terms for push are "emphasize" or "romance." Pull back on then means "to throw away," "off the cuff," not make such a big deal of, underplay.

There are a few different ways to push or pull, throw away or stress the importance of. Sometimes the copywriter will underline these words or phrases so you will know which words they want you to spend more or less time on.

There may also be direction given at the bottom which tells you what to emphasize or de-emphasize so that you have a guide to follow.

If they don't give you any direction, you need to go with your gut and see what comes out of the read after you have done your homework of the spot.

Below are some general technical guidelines for a commercial. After a while these things will be second nature, but for now, read and learn these guidelines:

The product name is pushed more (emphasized) than other words in the commercial.

The idea or main theme is usually given more attention than the throw away words like and, but, the, once, before, etc. This becomes easier to interpret the more that you read.

Don't over-analyze. Read the copy. There is usually a rhythm and way that will come naturally. You will begin to understand what to play with more or romance, and what to throw away or do "off the cuff."

Some copy will not have a rhythm. Everything cannot be written incredibly well. I still audition for things that after I'm through I say, "What???" But you just have to read it with the type of attitude that you think they are looking for. It doesn't always have to make sense and go with the product they are selling. Don't look for the most intelligent way to read the copy, and don't spend massive amounts of time romancing or pushing the copy. The most natural read to fit the attitude that you can find is the best choice. Sometimes if you over analyze, you lose the meaning. And you don't book the job.

ATTITUDE!

Now generally, copy is written with a certain attitude in mind. The writer and the client have approved the copy and want it read a certain way. This sometimes means that they will give you line readings and show you exactly how they want you to read the copy showing tone, timing, energy level, feeling.

So relax, have fun. Reading copy is a blast! There are so many different ways to read, that you are open to experiment. Treat it like a guide. Just follow along with what is provided, and begin.

☞ *You need to remember, if you are just auditioning or interpreting the copy for yourself, you cannot read their minds. You don't know EXACTLY what they want. Sometimes you will book the job and you will hit the nail on the head, and sometimes not. But remember, you just need to do your job. Copywriters hear things in a certain way, and that is up to them. If they book you on the job, they will tell you to emphasize certain words, or go up on a word or down on a phrase. That is considered technical and you, as the actor, cannot concern yourself with what you don't know.*

DIFFERENT WAYS TO SELL

Below are some different types of reads and sells and what they mean. Open your horizons for experimentation.

SOFT SELL

The soft sell is just a general term for a type of sell that is quieter, or more intimate. The read should be gentle, romantic, warm, caring, loving, womanly. This read could be done so many different ways, but this gives you a blueprint or beginning, from here you experiment. Here are a few products that generally ask for soft sell type of reads.

Lingerie, Cat food, Feminine Hygiene products, Makeup, Hair Products, "Sensitive issues", medical, dental, health issues.

But don't let the above confuse you, because each one could just as easily be a:

HARD SELL

Now, a hard sell is right at ya. No playing around! This is a tough, strong, assertive read. In the 70s, they were big on these, BUY! BUY! BUY! And in the 80s they made a lot of fun of the HARD SELL, but you still were being pushed with BUY! BUY! BUY! and in the 90s they just threw things in your face but acted like they didn't care, they got you on the subconscious level, the gut, but it was still BUY! BUY! BUY!! No matter what, it's a HARD SELL. The hard sell can be approached so many different ways. Loud, Soft, Strong, Relaxed, Angry, HAPPY, HAPPY HAPPY! The wording and the direction are what makes it a hard sell. That, and the product. Any read can be read as a hard sell, but it depends on the product and what the copywriter is looking for. That is your guide.

Example: Toyota end of clearance sale. Better get here fast!

FLAT READ

This means that you just read the product flat without energy and care. It is really a laid back read that is meant to grab the attention of the listener. This read is done very low voiced, low paced and calm.

Nothing effects you. Nothing is pushed. Very real, very everyday guy/girl. These are all just different approaches to a read. You can still read it so many different ways. Within the flat read, you can ad any number of adjectives. Flat with more energy. Flat but informative, flat with a smile.

Example: Tom Bodett-MOTEL 6 "We'll leave a light on for 'ya."

STRAIGHT READ

A straight read usually means business read or it can mean conversational. Straight read just defines how the ad agency wants to sell the product. You can read something straight yet informative. You can read it straight with a smile. Straight reads are usually when the advertiser just wants to sell you information. Period. It's a read though. And a deliberate one. A straight read may be to a more sophisticated audience. The advertiser isn't trying to hit you over he head with pushing you into buying. They are trying to talk you into purchasing, using your wisdom and knowledge. A flat read is very monotone and is a more character read. The business read isn't going to try to make you laugh; it's going to try to impress you with the product itself.

Example: Apple Computer, Mastercard, Oldsmobile

SEXY READ

The sexy read is just that, sexy. They are trying to pull you in with sex. Warm, relaxing, inviting, invigorating, nurturing, playful, teasing, cunning.

Any adjective you can come up with that helps you define sexy, works for that particular product the advertiser is selling. Within yoursexy read, use some of the adjectives above to deepen your read and give it more pull. This is how you ad life to your dialogue. Making choices. Specific choices within a general characterization.

Example: Folger's Coffee

HIGH ENERGY OR ENERGETIC READ

This read consists of using your energy. Your enthusiasm. You can certainly get any number of reads out of this, depending on vocal quality with your voice and level of excitement. This type of read lends itself to all types of interpretations. You can be energetic and fun. Energetic and relaxed. Energetic and conversational. Energetic and gregarious. Energetic and nervous.

Examples: Reebok, Toys Я Us, Carl's Jr.

CONVERSATIONAL READ

You will hear this term a lot. Advertisers love a conversational read. Why? Because they sound natural. A conversational read is exactly like you have in everyday life. Nothing is phony. Conversational reads are very natural and not planned or forced.

Examples: *Los Angeles Times*, Purina Puppy Chow,

A lot of radio copy will have the direction "conversational."

Conversational readswill also often call for other adjectives. Conversation and wry. Conversational and informative. Conversational and straight. Conversational and warm.

There are so many reads, I've only listed some that may come up in direction. The above are commonly used, so you should know them. Any of the following can be integrated into defining a read:

Off The Cuff
Wry
Dry
Warm
Authoritative
Intimate
Aggressive
Sophisticated
Informative
Somber

Certain products will be sold in a certain way. Different types of sells go with different products. Cars and wine are sold differently. But this also may depend on the type of car and the type of wine. The car ad could be intimate while the wine may be fun and hip. It's important to look at the copy and see the direction and the visual. Also read the copy a few times, get comfortable with what it says and then read it aloud. Interpret the type of spot it is by what the advertiser is saying. This is a good beginning to follow. Learn to distinguish the type of spot.

Comedic Read: AT&T, Got Milk?

Business Read: Blue Cross Healthcare, Secure Horizons

So you get the picture. The reads are simply ATTITUDES! Just read them the way that feels natural. I've just listed some to give you an idea of the ways to interpret the copy and begin to understand rhythm in the read.

Have fun!

"The most significant tool the voice-over performer has in today's competitive market is their own unique personality."
    —*Cindy Akers, owner, Voicetrax West Recording Services*

CHAPTER 6

•••

GOLDEN RULES, SUGGESTIONS
AND COMMON PROBLEMS

•••

How do I find the copy to read?
You don't. The copy goes from the ad agency to the casting directors and voice-over agents. Now, for non-union jobs, you just need to follow what I've said before and pound the pavement with the local production companies, radio stations and ad agencies. But for the union people, you need to meet your casting directors and agents to get the work.

Do I tell people my union status?
Yes. You can't lie, because all they have to do is to call the union and ask them if you are current. Current means on time, paid up and a member of the union. If you are booked for a job and aren't in the union or are not current you may be fined, as well as the ad agency for hiring you and you have a chance of ruining your reputation.

How do I pick the best agent?
It depends on who you can get or if you get to choose. In most cities the choices aren't that large. In smaller markets, and the midwest, you may only have 1 or 2 to choose from. Talk to them, find out if they get a lot of copy and if they are connected with the casting people and ad agencies in town. Make your choice from there. You may prefer to have a smaller boutique-like agency that can give you more attention and has less people or you may like the larger corporate style agency that has a little more power and may know more people. You have to decide what is best for you.

How long should I sign the contract for?

You can only sign for up to one year when you join the agency. Union rules. After the one year you can sign for anywhere from a year to three years. Standard if you have a good relationship with your agent is three years. If you are at all unsure, just sign a year at a time.

What is the commission that my agent gets?

Ten percent. By law, they cannot get any more. That is a standard union rule. They receive ten percent of all job checks that pass through their office, they take a standard ten percent of the gross. That is the way it works.

Can I do "under the table" jobs if I'm in the union?

No. Not if you are signed by an agency. Not legally, anyway. This means that you are taking a job that the agency didn't get you. If it's a non-union job and you get caught you can be fined by the union, even dropped and/or your agency may drop you. If it's union, the agency will find out and they will know that they didn't get you the job. The best way to handle this is if someone wants you for a job, tell them to call your agent and hire you. If it's not a scale job, talk to your agency. If you aren't union, they may negotiate a lower salary so you can still do the job.

Do I get paid for non-air, non-broadcast work?

It depends. If it is a union job, you will be paid even if it doesn't air. Your agent will negotiate according to union fees. If it is an in-house demo for an ad agency and it could mean big bucks if the client agrees to your voice, your agent may talk to you and see if you want to do the work for free. That is up to you. You should take advantage of certain opportunities that could lead to bigger paying jobs like this.

What about if the work they want me for is for charity or a non profit organization?

This work is free. This work is called a Public Service Announcement (PSA). It is up to you to take it or turn it down. If you are recommended for the job or you read and get it, you decide. It could be for a great cause and your voice attached is a nice quality. You can request a copy of the work for your demo tape. Talk to your agent.

What if I do a bad job on an audition or a job that I've booked?
Don't worry about it. We all have bad days. You can't go back in to read. You can read over in the audition if you didn't like what you did. Just tell the casting director. They will know if you need to read it again. Usually they will let you. But we can be a bad judge of what we think it should sound like or what we sounded like. Let another opinion be the judge. The casting director or agent usually knows what the client is looking for. They will work with you. If they are not unhappy, let it go. Don't make suggestions. A session can get frustrating, but usually it doesn't have to do with the talent. There is a lot of work going into the session. Remember, you are only one part of a large group that got to the point of the session. Make sure that you don't leave a session on a bad note.

The writer is worried about the director and so on and so on. You are all trying to get to the same goal: Do the best work for the product and the client. If you worry that the writer/director/client/producer doesn't like you, don't worry about it. Just go in, do the work they hired you for, and be pleasant. The session is usually a smooth process. You just may be in there awhile doing different reads. Just remember to be, there were a lot of people who you beat out for the part. So hold your breath, count to ten and begin again. You'll get through it, and walk away counting the cash. . . only you won't get the cash for a month or so.

When do I get the dough?
If you are represented by an agent, you will get the money through them in the form of a check about a month after the job. They will take out their ten percent before sending you the check. This is just a general time frame. The money could come to you in two weeks, but usually to get through all the channels, it may take longer. If you have been waiting for the money for a long time, call the accounting department at your voice-over agency and they will find out for you. If the money is over a certain amount of time, the client and agency will be penalized and you will get a late fee. Residuals come in groups. If the commercial ran seventeen times in a week, you will get a check when they put it together. The FCC follows how many times the commercial runs. If you are non-union, I suggest you get the agreed upon money when you are done with the job. I wouldn't let them mail it to you.

What If the check amount isn't right or they paid you for one job when you did three?

This happens. Call the accounting department and tell them. They may need to see a copy of the contract that you signed at the job. That is another reason it's important to keep your contract copy. As long as you signed that you did three jobs, they owe you for the other two. If there is a further problem, talk to your agent. They will straighten everything out so that you are paid the right amount.

Remember, when you are at the session, make sure that you sign the proper paperwork for the amount of work that you did. If you do more than what is on the paper, don't sign it until you speak to your agent or speak to the ad agency that is there with you or on the phone. Just make sure that you are paid for what you do.

If you aren't sure how many spots, tags or changes you did that you should be paid for, talk to your agent. Tell them or fax them the copy, they will know how many spots it is. You need to be paid for everything that you do. You can't pay the bills with favors!

What about callbacks?

Treat this the same as the audition. Go in and read. That's all. Your agent will let you know if you've booked the job.

How do I follow the trend of what the current "sound" is?

Don't worry about it. Worry more about doing "your thing." It'll catch on. Remember, the business is about personality. Just have one. And use it. There are trends all the time. The business goes through waves and cycles that change all the time. There will be times that you will be called for an audition to "sound like," "similar attitude to" and "try to be close to. . ." Just follow the direction. Do what you can within your range to copy the attitude that they are looking for. Don't change your voice to impersonate the person. If they want Rosie O'Donnell, they will hire her. But if they ask for a Rosie O'Donnell type of read, then follow that style of read. If they are looking for a Tom Selleck style, follow that. Whatever that means to the writer and to you as the voice-over performer.

Can I read the copy with other people if more than one person is in the spot?

At the audition, if you are already paired or grouped together and you all want to read it, go ahead. The casting director won't tell you to do that, but if you both or all want to read it together a few times, you can. That is up to all of you.

What if I see another epic of copy at the audition that I want to read for?

Sometimes, where you go to read, there will be more than one audition going on. They have called you in for a specific job and for a specific reason. If you see something else that you feel you'd be right for (and the direction fits your description), ask them if you can read. They may or may not agree to it. If you feel that you are being passed on, speak with your agent and let them know that you feel you aren't being sent out for everything you feel your right for.

How do I send out the tapes to people?

Send them in a cassette tape envelope. Make sure you include a note to the person receiving the tape.

How do I make sure that I am being sent out on all that is available?

How do I go out for more comedy, car ads, soap commercials, promos, etc. ? Go on all the auditions you can. Talk with your agents and let them know you would like to go out more in a specific area. If they have the connections and are getting the copy, you should be able to go in more in that area. They may recommend a class in that area to help you.

What about if I have a commercial tape, animation and promo tape? How do I know which to send where?

Very simple. Commercial tapes goes to commercial casting directors and ad agencies; animation tapes go to animation casting directors, animation production houses, and studios; and promos go to networks and production companies. You need to make sure that you at least have the commercial demo tape, and keep lots of copies.

Do I need more than one type of demo?

Not when you are just starting out. Even after that, if you work mainly in animation, that should be your primary tape. Your commercial demo tape is important and you should always have that with you. You can still book other areas of voice-overs.

How do I book more jobs?

Just keep auditioning. The more your voice is out there, the more work that you will book. That is the way that the business is. A leads to B.

How do I come up with different characters?

Play with your voice. Do what you can. The more you audition for animation, the more chance you will get to use your voices. These days, the animation bookings are more and more common. Listen to Saturday morning cartoons. See what's out there.

What if I can't make an audition?

Let your agent know. If you don't have an agent, let the company know. If you can't make it for whatever reason, try to reschedule for later or earlier in the day. Voice-over auditions are not held for two or three days in a row. Don't be a "no-show." Always call. It is a small community, and if you don't show, they will remember and consider you to be irresponsible. Keep your appointments.

What about gifts for clients?

During the holidays, you can send a basket or small gift. Keep up with your contacts. If you have regular clients, It's good to send a card but large, expensive gifts aren't necessary. A lot of people do a special voice-over demo holiday tape or a fun gift. Try to think of something that will stand out.

KEEPING TRACK OF THINGS

- *Send thank-you notes, new tapes and cards when you change agents. Occasionally send a "just keeping in touch" card.*

- *Keep your records filed in case SAG, AFTRA, AGENT or PRODUCER has a question, you have the information handy.*

- *Know around when you should be getting paid, (four to six weeks is about right. Some jobs can take up to eight weeks to pay. Anything longer than that, check with your agent or call the ad agency). Know what you should be getting paid and the cycle the spot is running so you can keep track of your money.*

- *Have a record of what would be a conflict for you/what other spots you have running.*

- *Keep a list so that you have some idea of what kind of spots you are going out on, reading for and places you are going.*

- *If you have questions for your agent, he can pull a job up immediately by your date, job, etc. (Also for SAG, AFTRA)*

AFTER THE SESSION

After your session, staple a copy of the contract to your copy with the time, date of the job, the ad agency's name and the writer's name and file it. The above information should be kept somewhere that you can readily find it. I have a friend who keeps everything on a computer. It's a great idea. I'm not that meticulous, but I do have all my jobs written down and dated from 1994. It's also good to be able to look back and see what kind of jobs you were getting, how the market has changed, and what kind of roller coaster your voice is taking you on. It also doesn't hurt to have past job information so you can re-send voice-over tapes. Even if they haven't used you in a few years, they may be just around the corner from some new campaign that you are perfect for!

DON'T FORGET

- Re-submit your tape to ad agencies, especially ones which have used you in the past.
- Keep your tape current. Add new spots as you book; take old spots off your tape that no longer apply.
- Put your "signature" voice first on the tape. The next spot should be as different from that signature voice, as possible. Show them your range.
- Send demo tapes to appropriate places.
- Send promo tape to appropriate places.
- Don't send a regular demo tape to an animation house and vice versa.
- If you don't have a promo tape, send an appropriate demo tape.
- Take an animation class with a casting director to get to know them and build a "stable" of voices.
- Don't waste money on an animation tape that isn't good. Make sure that you are ready, with lots of different voices. Take from real copy. Don't write your own.

The same advice applies to demo copy for a demo tape. If it's homemade, take from magazines, cut to time and make sure that it is good. Let someone else listen to it. Listen to the radio. Make sure that you sound real, and not like you are selling or pushing. Your voice should not overpower the product, it should enhance it.

If you do a homemade tape, don't overpower it with tons of music and background noise. Show what you can do with your voice than how musically enhanced your tape can be.

CHAPTER 7

•••
THE DEMO TAPE
•••

Demo tapes are a requirement within the voice-over industry. They are the only way to effectively show your vocal range, different attitudes and characters. They are your calling card and what you will need to get auditions as well as secure yourself an agent.

What is a demo tape?

A demo tape is a collection of your various commercials and/or voice variations condensed onto one tape; different styles, tones, and attitudes. It is what you use to sell your voice and show the agents, clients and ad agencies what you can do with your voice

How long should the demo tape be?

The demo tape should be between two and four minutes long. Professional voice artists' tapes are closer to four minutes long because they have more work to choose from. If you are just starting out and you have no produced reads, just put together your best five or six and keep it short—about two to two and one half minutes. Edit it to your liking and make sure that the tape sounds clear.

An animation tape should feature five or six different character voices. If you are just saying one line with each character, put a few more on—no more than two to three minutes. The same applies to promo tapes: keep it to under three minutes.

What should be on the tape?

Don't put too many different voices on the tape. Music is not essential but may help. Don't put the entire spot on the tape, unless you've only done a few commercials and that is all you have. Try to put different styles on the tape. Do not do five sexy reads, where every commercial sounds the same. If you feel you are strong at sexy reads, pick the copy best suited for that read. If you have a Coca-Cola spot and a lingerie ad, obviously your better choice for the sexy read would be Coca Cola. But it's important to understand what the ad is trying to say and trying to sell. Just because the lingerie ad is a sexier product, doesn't mean that the ad agency wants it to be read sexy.

> *If you are a deep voiced male and you don't know what to put on but you think you do a great "John Goodman/Good ole guy" type read, that's where you begin. Find copy that would be appropriate, and read that. Then use the strength in your voice for a hard sell for GMAC Trucks—for a second read. Push the read out, have fun with it. Then look for a straight man read. Something like a coffee commercial or a jeans ad. Be the regular guy. Conversational, relaxed. Then find a good husband piece of copy, (you can have a double-two people-in your tape, just make sure the double doesn't overpower your single reads and don't put it on first if the other person has the first line). Put one of those lovey mushy husband/wife spots in and then the next read should be dry, off the cuff, a beer commercial. You get the picture? So many choices!*

Should your demo tape be professionally edited?
The commercials should flow seamlessly, woven together so there is no separation. If you can afford to hire a sound engineer and a director to put together your demo tape, they will do that for you. Otherwise, if you are doing a homemade tape, you'll be putting the tape together yourself. Don't label each commercial before they come on. Announcing each product makes your tape sound choppy. Just put the commercials on the tape, back to back, and let them run. You want the listener to hear your voice in various reads, and you want the tape to flow smoothly. If music is already on the commercial, it can provide a nice background.

A demo tape is like a story.
Keep your listener interested. Don't put similar voices together. Break them up. Take the listener on a roller coaster ride. Most people listening to audition tapes will only listen to the first couple and move on to another tape. Keep them listening. Don't do anything zany like adding subliminal suggestions, just do the copy and do it well. Don't put all your winners up front and have the

back end weak. Keep the tape moving along at a nice pace. Keep it professional.

What about a homemade demo tape? And what about using fakes?

If you are just starting out and you don't have the money or the experience for the real thing, then do a homemade tape. I did my first demo tape at home on an old recorder. The quality wasn't so great but it got me non-union jobs. You need the non-union work to build up and get better.

When you are starting out, you can use your "fakes" mixed in with non-union commercials. Replace the fakes and non-union spots with your "jobs" when you get them. Even on a professional tape though, you may be using fake spots that you are directed on, to fill up your tape. Do not label the particular commercial as a fake. Don't worry about telling whomever listens, this is real and this isn't. You won't be asked.

Should I do impressions?

No. There is a difference between a "Rosie O'Donnell read," a "Tom Bodett read" (Motel 6: We'll leave the lights on for you"), the "Regular Guy read," the "Terri Apple read," the "John Goodman read" and a genuine impression or impersonation of those voices. You will never hear an impression of Sylvester Stallone, unless it's actually Stallone himself What you will hear are similarities to attitude. When they ask for a "Rosie O'Donnell read," they don't want you to imitate Rosie O'Donnell. They want you to copy the type of attitude that she has. Sarcastic,wry, tongue in cheek. Same for John Goodman. They don't want you to listen to John Goodman and sound like him, they want that type of read. Regular Joe next door, happy go lucky, hard worker, blue collar. You need to learn to interpret the types of reads these people represent. If they ask for a Demi Moore read, they want an off the cuff, raspy, woman of the world, early 30s type read.

Should I make up the copy?

No. Do not assume that you can write copy better than the professionals. Even if you don't like what you hear or read most of the time, the client has approved what the ad agency has done. That's why it's on the air or in the paper. No matter how creative you think you are, there is a rhythm and a reason that produced copy gets produced. Use copy from your auditions or from magazines. If you are being directed and paying for a professional tape, copy will be provided. You will go over what you are putting on the tape with the director. If you find a piece of copy you want to add, go over it with the director. Don't make up your own. It will come across as unprofessional.

Should I have someone direct me on the demo tape?

Yes, when you are recording a professional demo tape. If you feel you can do this yourself and want to save some money, rent a studio, hire an engineer and do it yourself. Be sure you know what you are doing, though. Otherwise this becomes costly and you might as well have hired a director to put the tape together with you.

You can find directors who will produce your demo tape through many sources: classes, casting houses, advertising agencies. Directors can also be casting directors, writers, producers and teachers. A casting director may also direct and produce demo tapes as well as teach classes.

A director will take the time to work with you to put the best tape together as possible. She will help you find a good "niche" for your voice. She will know a good rhythm for the tape, as well as where to add in music and sound effects. If you have some real spots that you've done, she will know where to put them in, if at all. She will take the time to work with you and get each read perfect. Your tape should last a while.

If you can find someone who knows something about voice-overs to help you with your home made tape, go for it! You will want a few people to listen to your tape and give their comments, before sending out for prospective jobs.

How much does a demo tape cost?

If you get one produced professionally it can run anywhere from $400 to $1,000. Demo tapes aren't inexpensive. They are the only tool that you have for this business, and you should be able to write it off (check with your accountant). Once you have a master copy of your tape, you can add new work on as you get jobs. The tape is good for a year or two depending on how much work you get in the meantime. This is your calling card. Make it the best you can.

Making a homemade tape will cost you for the equipment (microphone, new recorder, music) as well as the tape itself and copies. Invest in a good tape recorder and microphone.

If you rent studio time and do the work with the sound engineer without a director, you will pay for the time in the studio. Prices range from $45 to $150 an hour depending on the studio.

The sound engineer will do all the technical work and edit the tape to your specifications. In this case you are your own director. Plan to be there for at least five hours. The sound engineer will just be keeping timings of spots for you and putting this on a master. Then you edit it all together with them to get the finished product. You will then leave with the master and get copies made.

Do I say whether I'm in the union or not?

Not on the tape. Just have your name, phone number or your agency at the beginning of the tape or on your J-Card.

If you do not have an agent and are looking, you will need to specify your agency status when submitting your tape. Casting houses can then bring you in to audition for the proper commercials. You can still read for union commercials without being in the union. If you book one, you can join, so going up for union commercials does have its benefits.

Where do I make copies of my demo tape?

The studio where you recorded your tape can furnish them, although this is an expensive way to go. Or, you can call specific production houses that do duplicate cassette copying. This is definitely less expensive. The more tapes you get, the less each one will cost.

What is a master tape?

The master tape is gold! It is the original of your completed main tape. This is what you will use to make copies from, add on when you need to add commercials, and remove from when you no longer want a commercial on there. This is what you paid all that money for, so protect the master in a very safe place.

How many tapes do I need when I'm just starting out?

Twenty tapes should be a good start. You will want to hold on to about five for yourself to take around for future auditions and when you make new contacts. Send the others out to specific creative directors, production facilities, agents, and casting directors.

What do I do after I send the tapes out?

Wait a few days to allow time for the recipients to have listened to your tape and then call them see if they want to meet you. Don't bother the creative directors, though. They'll keep you in mind. You know that you've sent it out. They may not pull you in for an audition, or a job for a long time. It is your job to make sure they've received it, after that, you can't make them listen to it.

The casting people now have a copy. Just drop them a line or a new tape every three to six months, so they know you're there, hopefully they will eventually call you in. You don't need to make a new tapefor each mailing, this is just to let them know that you are around and available. Do the same with smaller production facilities. They are always looking for non-union or last minute talent for a radio spot or industrial film or local commercial.

Should I give tapes to my agent?
Yes. Once you're with an agency, you need to give them about fifty copies to start out. They will want to send your tape out to all the agencies and casting directors in town. If someone calls for a recommendation, they may want to pull the tape and send it. Check your supply and make sure the agency has enough of your tapes. Making copies takes a few days, so don't let them run out. You should still keep a small supply for yourself for your own mass mailings and general mailings.

What about mass mailings?
Here's how I do it. I keep the paperwork from all my jobs. Then I re-send current tapes to all the places. Or I look through and find ad agencies in my general area whom I've never met. I also check advertising agencies in neighboring towns and send them copies as well. Although I live in Los Angeles, I can get hired by a company in Orange County, or in San Francisco. I do this a couple of times a year.

What is a house tape?
The house tape is your voice-over agency's master tape that has samples of all the voices they represent. Usually made about once a year, this tape is constantly being submitted to ad agencies, producers, writers, TV stations, CD ROM and animation houses—anywhere that your agent can think of that might be able to hire you. The tape is usually divided into; Men and Women, Announcers/ Promos (Men and Women) and Animation (Men and Women).

When they request a copy of your work for the house tape, you will need to pull the best two minutes from your regular demo tape.

You will pay for all the costs needed to get your agent the sample of your work to be used on their house tape. This will cost you studio time and will probably take the sound engineer a couple of hours to re-edit your tape down from three or so minutes to two.

Your agent may only want one minute of your best work on the tape. This is going to take some creative work from you and the sound engineer. It may be tough deciding what should go on. If you are known for one particular spot or read, definitely put that at the beginning of your tape. Your agent may want to hear what you've compiled before it's completed. Call your agent from the sound studio and play it over the phone.

After you've got the completed version, bring that to your agent on a DAT (digital audio tape). They will then take everyone's copy and put it on the house tape. They will pay for the work from there. You will only need to pay for the sound engineer/studio and the copy to make the tape. If you have several tapes: Promo, Animation and Commercial, you will need to make separate house tapes for your agent. Follow the same steps that you did for the commercial tape.

How important is my demo tape?
Extremely important! Your voice-over tape is your resume, your calling card. It is what will get you work.

What if nothing on the tape is real?
When you are starting out in this business, nothing will be real. If you don't have the experience, and you've never booked a job, you don't have a choice. Just pick the best written copy and go for it. You will slowly build up to real things on your tape. There is a lot of work for non-union talent and a lot of responsibility once you're in the union, so enjoy the non-union jobs. It's a great way to build tape.

What do I do when I get a new job?
When you get a new job, get a copy of the spot from the ad agency. If the spot is finished, they will give you a copy while you are at the session. If not, they will send one to your agent for you. You can also give them your home address and ask them to send it to you when it's completed. They will let you know if there is a fee. Sometimes, ad agencies will charge $20 or so to mail you a tape, and sometimes it's free.

Add it on to your demo tape as you go. If you get a couple of jobs, wait until you've got all the copies, and then add them to your demo. Every time you go into a studio and work with a sound engineer, you will have to pay their minimum hourly charge, so make sure that you're not going in there every two weeks to add things. Take off old spots, or ones you don't like as much as you start booking more work. Put the new ones closer to the front so that you will sound current on your tape. You don't want old spots on your tape, unless they are spots that you are known for. Don't worry, if you don't have a lot of spots for your demo, if the read sounds good and it's getting you work and/or auditions, keep it on the demo tape.

How often should I redo my tape?

You should not have to redo your tape more than once a year, unless you are booking a lot of jobs. In that case, you may want to keep changing your tape around so showcase the current projects that are playing.

How many different tapes will I need?

You will need a commercial tape for commercials, a promo tape for promos or narration and an animation tape for animation. If you are mostly going for straight commercial but you do a few wacky voices, throw them into the mix for a regular commercial demo tape.

Animation and commercials should be separate. If you're going for promos and animation, do the same thing. Do a tape just with promos. For trailers (film, TV) make a trailer tape. Keep everything separate.

> *I have a promo tape, an animation tape and a commercial tape. They each have work from that area. Each is around three minutes long and are set up the same way. Each agent required that I get a tape of my work so they can submit me for the appropriate job. If my animation agent just sends out my commercial tape, the casting agent may hear it and say, "Yes, she's good, but can she do the voice for a ten year old boy?" It's important to show the range that you have through the tape that you give.*

Are there different agents for different areas of voice-overs and will they need a copy of my tape?

Depending on the size of the agency, you may have an animation agent, a promo agent and a commercial voice-over agent. They will each require a demo tape for that area if you wish to pursue that field within voice-overs.

A smaller agency may only have one or two agents. They may

cover all the areas of voice-overs. You should still have different tapes for different jobs you are pursuing. When you are starting out, this can be very costly. Pick one area of voice-overs and narrow in on that, first. After you begin to work, then spend the money and time branching out. You may find that you are highly successful in one area and work a lot less in the other. Put your energy into the area that you make money in.

Should I bring the tape to every audition with me?

No, unless it's a more current tape and they haven't heard it. If you are going to a casting house, they already have a copy of your tape. If it's a more current tape or a different tape (animation, promo) then, give it to them. Otherwise, just as long as they have a current tape, they don't need another one. If you go audition at the ad agency, leave a tape at the front desk. Don't bother the producer and director. They called you in, they have a copy already. But once you're at the agency, they may have a creative executive for another campaign that hasn't heard you.

ANIMATION TAPES

Follow the same guidelines for the commercial demo. Try to find copy that is cartoon like or take from auditions or create your own. The tape should be no longer than three to four minutes with your different voices.

PROMO TAPES

Your tape should be three to four minutes of all Promos. You should do different types of promo reads. "Evening news at 6:00," "Tonight on *Friends*, wait until the laughs begin," "German Shepherds, the truth among the pack."

TRAILER TAPES

The trailer tape should have five or six different trailers. Remember, most trailer voice-overs are done by men. Their voices sound more authoritative sound We have also be trained to think that men's voices are more businesslike than women's. The general public seems to respond more to male voices when hearing trailers for a movie or TV show.

This may change but for not you need to be realistic about trailers. They are done by a very small group of people. The market is tight and difficult to break into. It's not unattainable though, and if you want to try for them, do a tape and send it out to trailer houses.

LOOPING TAPES

The good news is: you don't need a separate looping tape. Your regular commercial demo tape is fine. The bad news: there are specific loop groups (see the Appendix for groups in Los Angeles), but most are in major cities, e. g., Los Angeles, New York, Chicago. Loop groups generally loop movies and TV shows, so you need to be in a city where they produce these shows.

DUBBING TAPES

This can be a little confusing. If you've done a lot of dubbing, you can put together a specific dubbing tape. However, if you're working a lot in this area, they already know you, so you won't need a separate tape. Just send your regular demo tape to the dubbing houses. A lot of times, you will be hired for dubbing because your voice is similar in tone to the person whose voice you will be dubbing.

AUDIO BOOKS AND NARRATION

For a narration tape you should be narrating different five or six stories through the tape. But only do this if you specifically want to do narration or books on tape. For audio books, you can just send your regular demo tape.

J-CARD

The J-Card is the cardboard cover that goes over the demo tape, underneath the plastic cover (seen from the side, it looks like a "J" folded into the cassette case). Check with your local duplication house as to where to get them done in your area. The J-Card is a fancy cover that helps your tape stand out from all the others. You can just have your name put on it or do your own design. Anything at all. Some people get cases for their tapes and some just have the tape plain. This is just the icing on the cake, to add to the tape and make you stand out more. Printing color J-Cards is expensive. The individual cost of them will go down when you order in bulk. The cost of printing J-Cards ranges from $.50 cents a copy to $2.00 for each one depending on color and type of paper and design.

The J-Card is not a necessity. You will have a label on your cassette provided that you will put the agent and your name on. The J-Card goes on top of the tape, under the plastic cover. You can also have your agent's name and number on the J-Card to make it easier to find you.

CHAPTER 8

• • •
CLASSES
• • •

The best beginning is to find a good voice-over class.

Which class? Which teacher?

What if I live in a small town?

How do I find the class?

How many classes should I take?

How much money should I spend on a class?

Where you live will help make your decision. If you live in a small town where voice-overs are harder to get, you may need to compromise and take an acting or diction class. You can find those within your local school, drama club or local acting school. Also, check with the local papers or Learning Annex guide (a national school that teaches very unique classes in all areas). Classes can also be found by calling SAG (Screen Actors Guild) or AFTRA (American Federation of Radio and Television Artists). They should be able to help you find classes that are available in where you live.

There are several types of classes. Learning Annex offers a one night intensive class taught by a local well known voice-over person. It costs approximately $40 and will teach basic information about the voice-over business. You may be able to play with real copy and a microphone if they've offered it within their class. (Different cities have different ways of teaching). Also, the Learning Annex has a longer workshop (four to six weeks) that emphasizes diction, breathing, working on interpreting the copy and vocal range. Call your local Learning Annex first to find out details.

Most of the classes listed consist of an ongoing class that specializes in a certain field. These classes generally run from four to eight weeks. For example: there are plenty of basic beginner voice-over. You'll learn how and where to stand (or sit), how to interpret copy, how to vocalize the copy, how to give different reads, add or take away texture from your voice. You'll have a whole lot of time to read alone and play along with other people. Some classes will give you a tape to take home with your completed work that you can use to practice and/or add on your demo tape at a later date.

More intermediate level classes will mix you with more professional students. Your work will be more advanced, the copy a little more difficult (longer copy, more intense copy, strong dialogue, accents, different texture than you would be normally used to). This is a great class to really get to work on your skills. Also, there may be guest speakers from advertising agencies, voice-over agencies, as well as working voice-over people, all there to tell you the "inside scoop" of the business. It's a great way to really learn the ropes from working pros. There are also specific classes in animation. From beginning to pro, you can learn how to come up with voices, how to manipulate your voice to try new reads, reading actual copy that is used for television animation and film animation, actually play, read and record copy from animated shows. You will also learn the ins and outs of the business, how to make your read as great as it can be. You'll be able to compare yourself with everyone else reading the same copy and what makes one read so much better than the other.

> *How do you tell a bad class? When I first moved to Los Angeles, I audited a class. After the class was over, the teacher told me that I would be charged $50 to audit! I said that was ridiculous. His class cost $650 and he told me that I needed a new tape, and that he didn't like the one I played for him. The new tape would run me about $1,000. First of all, I had all real copy on that tape. It would of been just re-arranging the copy the way that he thought would be better suited. I refused to pay him and I never referred him. You have to be smart. Call around and look around. Read this book. Read other books. Go on the internet. Call an ad agency. Call a casting director. Get referrals!! That is the key. Find out which are the best classes to take and why. You may only have one choice but on the other hand you may have several. The bottom line is, you take what you can afford. This career is not cheap. You may have to put in $500 to start out between classes, books and putting together a tape, but down the line your investment will be recouped after just a few jobs.*

If you've done a few voice-overs and you are in the class to learn and workout, then take the next level. Usually you will be in the class with ten or more students and you will be doing the class in a studio like atmosphere. Make sure that you are getting to work on the microphone and getting to read copy. You need to get comfortable with this, and the only way is to study and practice. Some classes may just sit around and read copy aloud. This is done in a very well known class in Los Angeles. It's a great way to learn to interpret copy and feel comfortable reading aloud.

All classes should give you a "workout" atmosphere, where you are given copy every week and go into the booth to read a loud, alone or with others. You will listen to copy and analyze. You'll probably read it a number of ways and with different partners. They will play the read back for you, give you pointers and let you go into the booth again to try a different read.

There are also on-going professional classes which are great for working voice-over people. Even if you work a lot, there is more to learn. The class is most likely taught by a voice-over actor, producer or casting director so they know what they are doing. And you will be working with people who are working. So they know how to book. They are in the "loop" and you will learn from them. This is a great class.

READ BOOKS

There are different books you can buy: animation, diction, acting, books on accents. The following is a list of some magazines and/or other ways in which to help you learn more information as well as casting notices and jobs available within the voice-over market. If you are just starting out, the college circuit is great training ground. They are always looking for a voice-over or narrator for a short film, commercial or radio spot that they need for a credit in that class. This will give you tape and a chance to work. You've got to start somewhere! Also, production facilities and production houses that do infomercials, industrials and commercials will always hire new talent. Great place to go without having a demo tape. Drop off your name and phone number, see if you can get an appointment to speak with someone to put you on an in-house list when they are ready to cast or make a home made demo tape so that they have something to keep on file that will remind them of your voice.

MAGAZINES

Ad Week

Ad Age

AudioFile Magazine (Great for Audio Books/Audioworld, CD-ROMS)

Backstage West

Backstage East

Hollywood Reporter

Daily Variety

College Newspapers

Entertainment section of newspapers

Local radio flyers or magazines

Internet under "voice-overs"

Animation Magazine

KidStar-Interactive Radio Magazine

All the above publications may not be available in smaller markets. *Ad Week* and *Ad Age* are sold nationally and are great magazines to read to keep up on what's selling, what product is with which company, and what's going on in the ad world. It never hurts to keep up on the latest trend and style.

CLASSES IN THE LOS ANGELES AREA

Michael Bell Voice Animated Workshop

Animation, TV series, specials, CD-ROM's and feature film animated work. Six-week classes. Limited enrollment. Call (818) 784-5107 for details and dates.

Michael Bell is a well-known and well-respected voice-over actor. He has done animation for *Homeward Bound 2*, *GI JOE* Series and Movie, *Scooby Doo*, *Jonny Quest*, *Voltron*, *Defender Of The Universe*, Nickelodeon, *Mina And The Count*, *Man With No Nose* and many more. Michael also has an extensive casting and directing background.

In his classes, you will learn how to be competitive in the audition process and acquire ability to sustain many characters. You will learn to paint the picture with your voice, test the limits of your vocal pipes and imagination, rediscover the fun of "eating the scenery." Michael will teach you to "discover who's hidden inside, get 'em out and make 'em pay."

Sue Blu, Blupka Productions

Casting director, owner, voice-over talent, producer, animation classes. Call (818) 551-0315 to check schedule. Classes not on-going.

Sue is a wonderful producer, casting director and teacher. Her classes are very highly regarded and really work on emphasizing animation. Working on characters and learning how to develop to lead to future work is her strong suit. She also has produced and directed many prime time animated shows. She is also a very prominent casting director in Los Angeles and is very open to new talent.

Sue is also the co-author of *Word of Mouth,* another excellent book on voice-overs that you may want to take a look at.

Jocely Blue

Well-known successful voice-over actress/commercial and animation. (818) 981-4645. Private and group. Commercials—all levels.

Carroll Voice Casting

Carroll Day Kimble, casting director, owner, producer, demo tapes, classes, on going, all levels. private coaching and group. 6767 Forest Lawn Drive #203, Los Angeles, CA 90068, (213) 851-9966

Carroll gets some wonderful copy and is very loyal to people whom she loves. She is an excellent, patient coach and casting director and is a great person to learn how to interpret copy from. She will teach you the ins and outs of the business, what "they" are looking for and how to learn to do the best which can lead you to book the job.

Elaine Craig Voicecasting

Elaine Craig, casting director, owner, director, producer, on-going commercial and animation classes, all levels. (213) 469-8773, 6464 Sunset Boulevard, Penthouse, Los Angeles, CA 90028

Elaine has been in business for years and her classes are some of the best regarded in town. She teaches all level groups and on-going group classes. She has a wonderful studio and works very intensly on bringing out your natural talents. Her animation classes are also well known. She is also a wonderful casting director that is constantly busy and looking for plenty of voices to hire.

Kalmenson and Kalmenson

Cathy and Harvey Kalmenson. Full roster of teachers. All level classes—animation and commercial. (818) 342-6499, 5730 Wish Avenue, Encino, CA 91316. Classes held in Burbank.

Kalmenson and Kalmenson teach the fundamentals to all levels of students. They also bring you into read when they think you are right for a job. Harvey and Cathy are very hard working and talented. They get wonderful copy and always work professionally, treating the talent with the utmost respect. I think that working in this kind of environment especially for classes, can do nothing short of enhancing your reads and opening many doors of opportunity. They are hardworking, honest and will bring out the best in your talent.

The Learning Annex
The Learning Annex offers on-going classes in Los Angeles, New York, San Francisco and San Diego. Call or check their web site at www.learningannex.com for schedules and classes in your area.

Lou Hunt
Coach, all level classes. (818) 763-4260. Class held also at The Voicecaster.

Frank Muller
The Audiobook Seminar
Frank is the most sought out narrator for audio books. He was dubbed the "King of audio books" by the *Wall Street Journal*. Frank has narrated more than 150 audio books. If you want to learn everything about the audio books or books on tape business, this is the class to take.

Seating is limited. Two four-hour sessions in Los Angeles. An overview of the audio-publishing industry. Creating an audio book in the studio, acting and directorial skills that are necessary for a great session. Work on text, acting and directing, narrative text, characterization and learning to interpret the author's intent. How to make and critique demo tapes, agents and AFTRA, Industry reference guides and information in print and on the internet.

Call (818) 702-6570 or e-mail to WaveDance@mindspring. com

You can also find out more about Frank Muller or audio books on the internet at: www.bitchen.com/muller or www.idsonline. com/terraflora/audio.

☞ *Pick up a copy of* AudioFile Magazine *to learn more about audio books.*

Radio Ranch

Dick Orkin, casting director, owner, director, writer, producer, on-going classes. All levels. Demo tapes. (213) 462-4966, 1140 N. La Brea Ave., Los Angeles, CA 90036. Classes held at another location

Great with classes. Learning how to interpret copy. Wonderful writer. Learn ins and outs of radio dialogue. He has written, directed, produced and performed commercial voice-overs for years. Taking the class helps your chances of booking out of The Radio Ranch. Wonderful with hiring actors he knows.

Tobias Communications

Maurice Tobias, owner, former casting director, coach. Demo tapes. On-going classes. (213) 939-8679.

The Voicecaster

1832 West Burbank Boulevard, Burbank, CA 91506.

One of the biggest casting houses. Calls in all level of talent and has a very large pool of people who they will continuously call in to read. Great place to book work out of. Lots and lots of copy. Very actor friendly. Okay to drop your tape off.

Kat Lehman's Workshop

Well-known class for all levels. Great way to learn the "biz" from an inside perspective. Uses real copy and will help land you in the door at Voicecaster. Coaching. Demo tapes, on-going—all levels. (310) 594-4871. Classes held at The Voicecaster.

Avery Schreiber

Actor, director, v/o actor, known for comedy. Improvisational workshops and performance relaxation. (818) 989-4775. Classes held in Santa Monica (also works with Second City in Toronto, Chicago, Los Angeles and Detroit).

Voicetrax West

Cindy Akers, owner, producer, director, coach—private and groups, all levels. Demo tapes. (323) 850-1112, 3611 Cahuenga Boulevard West #A, Los Angeles, CA 90068.

Beginning, Intermediate, Advanced Commercial Workshops; Advanced Commercial Casting Director workshops; Advanced Trailer/Promo Workshops; Advanced Animated Casting Director Workshops; Private Study (Before an audition, working on skills, one on one).

Cindy is a very good coach, director and producer. Her boutique production and casting facility offers great animation classes, as well as celebrity classes, where she'll pull in some of the top working voice-over talent to teach on a specific night. Great way to learn the tools of the trade and learn from a pro. Nice, cozy environment with smaller classes so that you will get more one-on-one attention.

Susan Silo Animation Classes
Very talented voice-over actress as well as on-camera. Coaches on and off. Great class to be a part of and play around to learn new voices and how to manipulate your voice. Learn from a pro on how to get into doing animation for a living.

Highly esteemed and accomplished cartoon voice-over actress. On-going private sessions—call for details: (310) 828-8767. (Some cartoons include: *The Smurfs*, *Captain Planet*, *Felix the Cat*.)

Voices
Mary Lynn Wissner, casting director/owner/producer. On-going classes—all levels. Demo tapes. (818) 980-5659, 4051 Radford Avenue Ste A, Studio City, CA 91604.

Well-respected casting director. Teaches on-going classes. Gets lots of great copy and is willing to see new people and help mold careers.

Dave Sebastian Williams Workout Workshop
Voice-over talent, coach, all levels, near Universal Studios. (213) 960-7833. Pay per class. On-going.

Chris Zimmerman and Charlie Adler
Casting directors—very well-respected and knowledgeable. Animation classes. Hanna Barbera, 3400 Cahuenga Boulevard, Hollywood, CA. 90068, (213) 851-5000.

Loop Groups in the Los Angeles area

Sandy Holt, Loop Ease
Owner, Producer, Director, Actress, Looper, Coach. For more information on classes and loop group, call (310) 271-8217.

An Interview With . . .
CORY WEISMAN, Top Animation Agent

Cory started out in Chicago in the music business, moved to Los Angeles, became a talent agent and then moved into the animation field as an agent. He represents and has negotiated some of the biggest features, television series, CD ROM's and celebrity contracts. He is one of the most well known agents in the industry.

Can you name a few of the projects that you have put your clients in?
Some or them are: *Toy Story, Babe, Space Jam, Homeward Bound 2, All Dogs Go To Heaven 2, Hunchback of Notre Dame, Mulan, Antz, The Prince of Egypt* and *Rugrats*. Lots of TV Series, CD ROM's, live action features.

What is a "live action feature"?
Live action means not animated. *Babe* is a live action, *Jungle Book 2, Whispers* (A Disney live action with elephants). Voice-over actors are used to create the voices and personalities of the animals appearing on the screen. Since *Babe* did so well, the market for live action features has really opened up.

You have been known to say that you love good actors. . .
I love good actors who are good people to work with, too. I may have ten actors who are right for any given part. I want to get them all in to read for the part. I want everyone to have a good year. If they call about a certain voice, I may have five or six actors or actresses who can book the job. My job is to sell them to the producers.

You have a great relationship with all the casting houses and producers in town. They all love you!
Good relationships are very important. Knowing everyone and keeping up on castings, knowing what is currently working, producers, it all helps.

Do you have a lot of working clients?
Yes. Some clients work six to eight jobs a day. I have a handful of actors who can do any voice, match any voice out there. I know that they could do any job well.

Can you tell me about CD-ROM's?
The CD-ROM market has narrowed down. They have consolidated. At the beginning, there were thousands of companies, there were too many titles, the market got oversaturated. There are now a lot of great CD-ROM companies, but not as many independent games produced. I book both celebrity and non-celebrity voices for a lot of CD-ROM's. I just booked James Woods on a CD-ROM and Kathleen Turner on another.

How many clients do you have in the shows that are currently on TV and in film?
It varies from series to series. Our clients have a very strong presence in almost every series produced here and abroad. Worldwide markets as well, feature films and interactive.

Do celebrities get most of the animation work?
Celebrities will book the lead roles on features a lot of the time. Their names are used to market the big budget animation films. But some of the most talented and versatile actors who we represent are non-celebrities who specialize in the art of voice acting.

How do you feel about demo tapes?
The best calling card is a good tape. Either you should put the tape together with a producer who can help you create different characters, write the copy, get the copy from casting directors, or find a tape producer who will help you find copy that is right for the characters that you want to put on your tape. If you don't have a good demo tape, it makes it harder for me, as the agent, to get you in to meet the casting directors and producers. I may need to play a tape over the phone at the last minute for a producer, if you don't have a tape, you may miss out on the job. If a producer or casting director calls me to see five or six people and you are the one without the tape, or someone else has a better tape, I will suggest them for the job.

How do you feel about classes?
Take a class, first, before trying to get an agent. Always good to

brush up in classes and hone your skills. You want to appear competitive. The way that the business has evolved, there are so many new casting directors and so many new projects, you have to have a tape. I do business with New York, Chicago, Japan, Australia, New Zealand. I need a tape to compete in those market places.

What do you look for as an agent?
Most agents don't want to develop you as the talent, they want to market you. You need to put your best foot forward. Our main job is to take the skills that you have and sell you. A lot of actors have their own specialties. Certain people are known for doing certain characters.

Do you work with anyone in animation in other languages?
I do a lot of foreign looping. Japanese and French animation. Foreign dubbing. Film actors do very well in dubbing and looping because they do a lot of ADR for their own movies. They learn to lip sync and loop really well.

What other markets are there within animation?
The market has expanded so much. There is animation - Saturday morning, prime time, specials, features, live action features, live action sitcom, CD-ROMs, looping/ADR, audio books, voice-overs for TV series and so much more. There is a lot of work out there, in many different areas of animation.

We get a lot of calls for voice-overs for *Seinfeld, Cybill, Home Improvement*. The voice coming from the television or speaker. A thought coming from a dog. Theatrical voice-overs. The world of character voices. They use a lot of character voice-over people, not necessarily "cartoony" voices. If an actor is versatile at creating character voices, you can open up the. There are so many other outlets within character voices now.

Can you talk more about classic characters?
Classic characters can be "Winnie the Pooh" (voice of Jim Cummings), or even a current classic that just starts out doing a series and develops over time, such as "Tommy Pickles" in *Rugrats*. E. G. Dailey is the voice of Tommy in the feature as well as starting the voice on the TV Series. Now that the show has become so popular, it can turn into a franchise: feature film work, live action, theme park voice-over use, CD-ROM, talking toys, commercials. It can be

CLASSES • • •

very lucrative for the voice-over actor. The classic character is one in which the voice is the only voice who does the character. It may branch out for years with everything from cartoons to the doll. The actor will make the money on it as long as the product sells.

Is the market changing? Is there a market for cartoony and real character voices?
There is a market for both. In the beginning, they wanted a lot more cartoony types, a lot more far out type of voices. There is more of a market now for people who can create a more human type of character voice.

CHAPTER 9

• • •
THE AGENT
• • •

Congratulations! If you've made it this far, you're doing well. Looking for an agent can be a difficult process.

THE AGENT'S ROLE

The agent is there to send you out on the most auditions, help land you the right jobs, and keep you working in the voice-over industry. The agent works closely with ad agencies, casting directors, and you, the voice-over talent, to keep up on what's being cast and getting the best material for their clients.

Following are some typical scenarios of getting hired.

Specific Request

A client or ad agency will ask specifically to hear you read. They will send over the copy/script and your agent will call you in to come in and read in the agency's recording booth. They will then listen and play it for the client who will decide if they want to hire you for the job. They may give the agent direction on how to read the copy, or they may just say, "Have her do her thing." If you are an experienced voice-over person, you will understand that "doing your thing," means giving them your "trademark" read.

☞ *Depending on how your agency operates, you may want to use a pager so you are always available when they need you. A last minute job can come in and you may be the one who gets hired, or miss out if they can't reach you.*

Group Request

The ad agency may call and say, "We're going to send over this copy for M & M's and we want to hear six of your best men who can sound like the guy next door in their late 40s. It's the agent's job to bring in six of their pick for this. Now, this doesn't mean that 25 clients couldn't do this particular read. I'm sure that they could. The agent will base it on giving the ad agency the best six. If they agent can throw on a few more, he will. The ad agency may have called three or four other agencies as well, to read clients. When they get the audition tapes back, they will listen and decide who to book for the job.

Specific Request and Group Request

An ad agency or client may call the agent and say, "I'm faxing you some copy that I would like to hear Terri Apple on, but could you also put another three or four women on who are similar?" Don't panic! Let me explain. Just because they like your voice, does not mean that they've sold the client on hiring you. They want to hear how you sound for that particular spot and may want to give the client other options.

When you go into your agent to read, they will tell you that you've been requested by a client but that other people are reading on the spot as well. At this time, do your best read within what they are looking for. If you're worried that they are typecasting you and you can do a different type of read, do it once you are in the booth. Tell the person running the casting session that you want to do a couple of different types of reads. Whatever read you do will be sent to the agency together with the work from the other ac-tresses. You will not be able to hear the other reads. This is part of the audition process and you should only worry about yourself and what you can do. Don't try to copy anyone. Work from within your-self, within your own personality, to create a unique and original read. This is what will set you apart and keep you booking the jobs.

Urgent Request

An ad agency or client may call your agent and say, "I have this radio or TV spot that I need a raspy female on, who can you get me by 3:00 today?" At that point, the agent will see who's available. (At my agency, if you are not available on any given day or week, you call in as soon as you know and they book you out on a board. Then if you're called by a casting house or ad agency for an audition or job, they will know to say that you're unavailable. Once you've booked out, the audition is gone. Casting houses do not wait to pull you in when you get back in town the following week.) Auditions go quickly and so do jobs. This is why it's very important to use a pager and be available. Most working voice-over artists rarely leave town very often. They know that a big job may be just around the corner and one day out of town means that you could miss the audition.

Auditions and jobs can happen 7 a.m. to 10 p.m. depending on when the ad agency schedules the session. Weekends are free time and you're okay to travel, although occasionally there's been an animation job on the weekend.

Back to being available. The agent will call whoever is around that would be right for the job. A specific name may come to mind when the ad agency describes what they are looking for or the agent may suggest someone they think would be right. You may hear the term, "Throw you a job," which is exactly what the agent has done. They may also give you the job if they have the option, because you haven't worked in awhile and they think you need it. These are rare occurrences. Most of the time, you will audition and be sent out or called to read.

General Auditions

Casting directors will call the agents when they have copy/scripts for the talent to audition for. Your agent will call you whenever, whatever time of day, they get the call. That is why it's best you make this your nine to five job.

> *Being available is tough. In the beginning, I had to wait tables at night and work part time at a talent agency. I still had to sneak away in order to get to the auditions. I didn't want to miss a potential job. You have to audition for the commercial. Your agent cannot call and try to talk the casting director into hiring you, the casting director is the mediator between you and the job. When the casting director gets the auditions, they send them to the ad agency to be listened to.*

The casting director will tell your agent who they want to see for a particular spot. Casting directors have many lists and many voice-over tapes. They keep them filed so they know who to call. The agent has already sent individual voice-over tapes and/or their house tape to the casting director, so they will have a full list of the agent's talent roster. If the agent feels that certain voice-over people aren't been pulled in, they will mention it to the casting director.

THE AGENT • • •

The casting director, just like the agent, may have a limit to how many people they can put on the audition tape.

Agent Push
The agent may call the casting director(s) and ad agency creative director(s) to let them know about a new talent they've signed. The agent may push to have that client read for a particular product. They will mail your demo tape to all requests that come in as well as submit your tape often to all ad agencies, casting houses, promo houses, producers and production companies. It is there job to keep on top of which ad agency has which product, who is casting for what and generally keeping smooth relationships with the casting directors so they will be sure to call in that agency's talent when they have something.

One-Stop Shopping
Some ad agencies will send copy/scripts directly to the agent. They do this for a few reasons. They may know the talent that they are looking for and it's at one particular agency, so why send it out to casting directors when they've just cut down on the time of the audition process? If an ad agency can hire all the talent for the spot(s) at one place, it saves them a lot of time and they don't have to pay the casting director to do it for them. They will call the agency and hire directly. You will be called into your agency to read for any and all copy that your agent thinks is right for you. Your agent will call you or page you to schedule a time for you to come in and read. You may have to negotiate your time if you have other auditions besides your voice-over agent. Let your agent know all other appointments as soon as you know them, so they can work around your schedule. They like to know that all talent is readily available so they don't have to call you every five minutes to check your availability. Most agencies will assume you are available if you have not booked out.

THE COPY AND YOUR AGENT
The copy that your agent gives you to read when you go into the office comes from advertising agencies, studios (promos, animation, narration) or producers who work freelance (i. e., not tied to a particular agency—just working for a client for an individual product, on a product to product basis. They move from one client to another). The agent receives the copy/script when it arrives (faxed, messengered, e-mailed or overnighted). The agent then

makes several copies of it to give out to the talent. If direction has been given to the agent, they will write it on the script or tell you.

Chances are slim that you will read for the same copy/script at your agency and then at a casting house. The only time I've known this to happen is when an ad agency didn't get the type of read they were looking for and had to send out the script again. They may have decided to hire another casting house or change from sending it to the agency to a different casting house. Many casting houses are on friendly terms with ad agencies, so they get a lot of copy. Different casting houses will get different copy. So will different voice-over agents.

Your Agency Contract

You usually sign with an agency for a year. After that, they may want you to sign for longer (two to three years), but it is best to re-negotiate every year. You want to make sure that you are happy where you are and the company continually works for you. If you are being "shelved" and not being sent out, you may want to have a conversation with the agent. You may find out that they don't feel that secure about you, in which case you may decide to depart after a year and go to another agency. If you were signed for more than the year, you would have a problem getting out of your contract.

The only way to get out of a signed contract, is to not book work in a three month period. If you've not booked a job within three months, the agent, legally, has to let you out of your contract so that you may pursue other options or agents. If you are called for a job, but turn it down, the agent does not have to let you out of your contract.

Your Money and Your Agent

Standard union rules state that your agent gets ten percent of every job that you do. This includes residuals. Simply put, every time you do a job or it re-runs, they get ten percent of whatever check you receive.

Even if you get a job through other sources (on your own—through other contacts, friends, business associates, boyfriends, mothers, agents, lawyers or the president) you are still required to pay your agent their ten percent fee because you are under contract with them. As long as they have you under contract, you cannot work for another agent or work non-union jobs. Some agents will represent non-union talent, but it really depends upon how much time and work the agent has to put in to develop newer talent.

Your agent is your protector. He will negotiate all aspects of the deal when you are hired for the job. He will work on getting you the best fee for the work that you do. Through the union, there is a base fee that the ad agency pays you ("scale"). Depending on level of work, years in the business and if you've got a lot of things running, you agent can negotiate a higher fee. Talent who works more, often gets paid a little more. This is the agent's job to negotiate. If you feel you've been working for scale for too long and want to be paid more, speak with your agent. Work together to get you the best money for particular jobs. A lot of very well known talent still works for scale because the competition is tough and ad agencies know they can get any number of voice-over artists for that job.

The agent will re-negotiate "holding fees" (the fees an agency pays you when they are not sure whether or not they will broadcast your commercial. These fees prevent you from recording commercials for competing or conflicting products.)

Show You the Money

When your check has been generated by the agency, it sends it to a payment service, which then sends it to the accounting department of your agency, which then deducts its ten percent commission, and sends you the balance. Sometimes the check is sent to you directly. When you receive that check, make sure that you call the accounting department of your agency and let them know you've received the payment directly. Then write a check for ten percent to the agency and send it to them. If you don't, or if you forget, the accounting department will deduct it from your next check.

When the Agent "Pockets" You

If an agent takes you as a "pocket client," they will not sign you to a formal contract, but, rather, will send you and your tape around first to see what kind of response they get. Even if you are very talented and work a lot, different agencies may not want to bring in a lot of the same kinds of voices. If an agent agrees to pocket you, they will treat you as if you are a client for that period of time, until they decide to either sign you or let you go.

You may be pocketed with more than one agency. Usually, agents will not like your being with more than one so they can exclusively make calls on your behalf. In New York, you can have more than one agent, but everywhere else, they like you to have only one. New York has a different system set up and they allow you to have as many agents as you want. Whichever agent gets you the job, gets the fee.

WORKING WITH YOUR AGENT

In voice-overs, it's extremely competitive and difficult to get to an agent. If one wants to take you on with a trial basis/pocketing, let them. See what they can do for you, as well. This is your time to make sure that you are a good match and they get you out on the kinds of things that you think you would be right for.

Also understand that your agent cannot get hold of every piece of copy out there. There are far too many agencies and far too many cities, not to mention tons of talent. So, how do you know if your agent is doing a good job? It's a tricky question. If your agent is well respected and known within the industry, ask around. Ask talent who works for them. Ask them how often they get out to read? Ask them what kind of copy they read for: Radio? Television? National Campaigns? Animation?

Also, in smaller towns, you may not have much of a choice. It just may be that the one or two agencies in town don't get much copy because there isn't much to get.

When I lived in Kansas City, I certainly didn't read five scripts a day. I was lucky if I read five a week. Smaller markets don't get as much copy. There are several other smaller markets though, depending on the advertising agencies, that do get a lot of national copy and will hire straight from their local town. In that case, that local agent will get the copy and fax it directly to your agent in that town. I still booked national spots in Kansas City because we had a terrific ad agency, BERNSTEIN-REIN, that had a lot of big accounts. Whenever there was something to audition for, I got a chance to read for it. The larger agencies may also send copy to large cities and large agencies so you may have more competition. But just because someone lives in a large city, doesn't mean they have more talent, just more opportunities.

When you meet with an agent, ask questions:
- Do you get a lot of copy? What kind of copy?
- How many other voices similar to mine do you represent?
- Where do you see my career heading?
- Do you think I can get out for animation? Promos? Narration?
- Do you think if I sign here, there will be too much competition with other voice actors?
- How many agents are there?
- Do you have a separate departments for animation, promos?

• How often do you think I'll come in to read?
• How often will I be going out to read?

An agent will not want to represent you if they don't think they can get you work. It's not worth it to them. They have many other clients they have to get work for. There is no guarantee you will work, even with an agent. The agent will get you in the door. You have to do the rest. They can push you for a job or get someone to meet you and hear you read, but they can't make that person hire you. That is up to the client and your read.

Your agent can set up appointments for you to meet casting directors, but the casting director will only see you if they have something for you to read. They may send you with your demo tape when you have an audition, or they may send the demo tape over, have the casting director listen, then bring you in to read for something they are casting.

Once you sign with the agency, get them copies of your demo tapes. An agency cannot take you on without a demo tape because they will need something to send out. They may take you on and send you on a few auditions, but you will need to get a tape done as soon as possible. If you don't have a demo tape, and the agency still likes your voice, they may bring you in to read some copy at the office. They may also discuss pocketing you or sending the audition out with the other actors to see if you got the job. The agent may pocket you for awhile without a demo tape and see if they can get you some auditions or jobs.

FINDING AN AGENT

Call SAG and AFTRA first for a list. They will send it to you. (You can also check their web sites as well for current lists of agents.) Look through your local yellow pages under talent agencies; go to your local book store look for directories in the performing arts section; call the local union, local production companies, local advertising agencies. Call a casting director in town; take a class; ask everyone you know in the voice-over field; call local on-camera commercial agents and see if they have a voice-over division. Check on the internet. Check with your local film commission.

Call the creative director at an ad agency, they may know of a few agents in town. In smaller towns you may only be able to choose from a few agents. Call them up, send them your tape and ask to set up a meeting for representation.

Check out reputations, talk with people who have worked with the agents and clients. Talk to your union to be assured that they are reputable. You want to be with a hard working agency that is making phone calls. You want to make sure that you are being submitted for all jobs. In every town, I'm sure there are bad agencies. A lot of smaller agencies in smaller towns, don't even have a voice-over department, so you will need to do some checking around. Then again, there may only be one agency in your town that does have a voice-over department, so you won't have much of a choice where to go. If they are signatory with the union, they have to follow the rules like every other agency.

Changing Agencies

If your contract has expired and you are not happy, you can leave the agency with no obligation. If, however, your contract has not expired and you are unhappy, then think seriously about changing. However, before you make that decision, make sure that you aren't frustrated just with yourself. Make sure that you feel the agent isn't doing what you think they should be doing. If they really aren't getting you out, you're not booking jobs when you used to all the time or they seem lazy in their attitude toward you, go talk with them. Maybe you'll find it's your attitude or a miscommunication. It's your job to make sure you get what you want from that agency. Here's a little advice to help give them a push before you heave ho it completely:

- Set up a meeting and talk about strategies.
- Ask them why you're not getting out as much as you used to.
- Make a list of clients you've worked for in the past that they could call.
- Be extra nice and always on time.
- Sit and listen to your tape as a group. Analyze it. Make changes.
- Have agents listen to your auditions. Analyze them.
- Gently push them into opening their view on kinds of voice jobs you can do.
- Make a tape with animation voices for them to hear.
- Get an animation tape made so they take you seriously to bring you in for animation auditions.
- Do a mass mailing yourself of demo tapes. Meet five new creative directors by sending tapes to unknowns.
- Don't complain.
- Impress your agent by taking a class even if you feel you already know everything.

- Be the first to arrive at the office for an audition. Don't be difficult.
- Be willing to change your demo tape if they don't like it.
- Tell them how serious you are about making this a full time career commitment.
- Ask them what else you can do to help your career along.

Try making all these changes first and seeing what kind of response you get. I would give them three to six months and see if anything changes, if not, and you are still not satisfied, change.

If your contract is up and you're still not happy, call around, set up meetings or have some casting directors that know your work get you meetings. Meet as many agents as you can. You want to make sure that you and your agent, realistically, want the same for you. Every voice-over actor wants to make a million a year. There are always steps to take. You want to make sure your agent is pushing you and believing in you. Maybe you weren't happy with your last agent because you lost out on a few national commercials that you didn't get to read for, but found out that the copy came in through your agency. They just didn't call you in. Or maybe you weren't getting out enough to other places. This can also be the casting companies. Unfortunately, your agent doesn't hold all the cards and sometimes it's a crap shoot. That's why I stress that it's so important that you have a current tape, be available and ready to work or audition. When you meet the new agent, find out what kind of copy they get in the office. Tell them if you want to pursue more animation, but your other agency wouldn't send you out. You may be better off at another agency. Maybe the last one was too big and you got lost. Maybe it's too small and they didn't know how to market you properly. The agent needs to know how to market you, sell you, get you out there, so make sure that you are on the same wavelength. If you want to start auditioning for promos and you have a demo tape, make sure they are willing to help you pursue this. They should try to help you break into new areas and be receptive to your ideas. You are signing a year of your life and income away, you want to make sure that you aren't sitting on a shelf somewhere waiting to be dusted off.

What You Can Expect of Your Agent

The agent's job is to help get you jobs, market your voice and make sure that the "powers that be" know who you are.

They are responsible for sending you out and making sure that you are reading for all the possible jobs that you can. They will make calls to submit you for jobs and send your tape around to casting directors to keep bringing you in for auditions. When you book a job, they will negotiate the rate and discuss with you if a job sounds shaky and you maybe shouldn't take it. Agents have lots of clients. You may be a top booker (Do a lot of jobs) or the agent may have to work harder for you, making phone calls, getting casting directors to see you on certain reads. The agents job is difficult because they have to push you and get you the work. Very rarely, even if you're famous, will you automatically get jobs just with a phone call. Sometimes an ad agency will call and hire you for something because they know you, but the agent does a lot more than just sit on the phone cold calling all day. They call around to producers, writers, directors, casting houses they know and will work on pushing you for a job, but it also comes about from sending out your demo tape, the house tape and constantly auditioning. The agent will pull you into the office, where a studio is set up, and have you read copy that has been sent from the advertising agencies. You will be put on tape and that read will be submitted. The agent will also do their best to make sure that your reads are up to par and suggest any changes that you can make to enhance your reads and get more jobs. They may suggest a class or a different demo tape. They want you to be the best that you can be.

It is your job to show up on time at auditions and be available. If you have an occasional question, call your agent. Don't call everyday with a gripe or wondering if you got a particular job. If you got the job, they will call you. Plain and simple. Sometimes, the toughest thing about voice-overs is wondering if you got the job. You may have a week where you read for twenty commercials. Just move on. If you booked any of those jobs, your agent will call you with the booking. You may also have weeks where you have no auditions. This is normal. Every week is different and it depends on the advertising world, not your agent. Your agent has nothing to do with how the advertising world runs. As long as your agent is connected and usually gets good copy, there's nothing you can be. The ad world goes through slow times, usually the last of the summer months, July and August, right before the rush of fall. The beginning of the year can be slow as well. Don't worry, it always picks up.

How Often Should I Call My Agent?

Should I say, never? Listen, the truth is, agents want you to let them do their job. That's an inside tip. You have to do what you want to feel comfortable and not left out of the loop of auditioning. If I wasn't auditioning, I would of never gotten any jobs, so someone had to believe in me enough to send me out. That's how it starts. Someone hears your voice on a demo tape, likes you and takes you on. Build your relationship with your agents very carefully. Make sure that your personalities are working together smoothly. You don't want to annoy your agent and call everyday: "How's it going?" "How's my career," "Why didn't I get those last ten jobs?" "Why didn't you get me in for that BLEACH commercial I heard on TV, that voice sounded just like mine?"

First of all, your agent may not have gotten the copy for bleach. You never know if the bleach commercial was cast in your town or not. Don't accuse your agent, assume they are doing their best for you. As far as asking about why you aren't booking as much or how about those last ten jobs? Call. Set up a meeting. Maybe for the next few auditions you go into the office for, your agent should listen before they go on the audition tape. Let them offer helpful hints on how you can improve upon your read. They may suggest a class. It may be a simple solution of making your reads more intimate or warming them up.

Sometimes, we have no control over changes in the ad world. They may like one sound for awhile, move on to another and come back to the original. Sometimes you just have to hang in there and keep reading. Calling your agent everyday to "check up," will only make your agent mad and consider you high maintenance.

You should call into your agency once a week. This is a good number. I'm not saying do this every week. Assume that your agent knows you're a client and give them a chance to work for you. If you feel you've been overlooked and it's been a few weeks since they've called for you, give them a call. Talk to an assistant. Ask for the agent. Just say something like, "Hi, It's Steve Jones. Just checking in. " If the agent says your clear, this means that they don't need you right then. If you feel that you've been forgotten and you signed with this agency, but never go in to read, set up a meeting, talk with the agents. You may be better off at a smaller agency where you will get more attention. Sometimes it's better to be a bigger fish in a smaller pond.

How Many People Work at an Agency?

It depends on the size of the agency. You may have one or two agents and one assistant making all the calls (this is called a boutique agency. It's a smaller agency) and doing all the work.

If it's a large company there may be three or four agents and many assistants. There also may be a separate animation agent, a promo/narration agent and a commercial voice-over agent. They are all there to help you get work. Keep them current on your tapes and do the best readings that you can do. Set up a meeting with your agent if you feel you're not as strong in an area, or your feeling frustrated. They may recommend a class, or tell you that it's slow now or your work is missing something. Ask advice!

What If I Hear Of An Audition That I Haven't Been Called For?

It depends on if you heard about the audition and it's at a casting studio. If that happens, call your agent and ask if they can possibly get you in on that. They may call the casting house and ask. Just because and audition came through to that casting house, doesn't mean they always call your agent. They may have filled their list of people and can't call anymore. If you are at a reading at that casting house already and you see other copy that you feel you'd be right for, ask the casting associate or casting director if you can read for the other project. More often than not, they are very nice and willing to put you on. Your agent cannot possibly know of EVERY audition in town. They can only do so much. The casting companies and ad agencies have to call them, as well as your agent putting in the calls. If you hear of copy/script at your agency that you didn't get to read for, this is a tricky situation. You want to be careful in calling. You don't want to undermine your agent. Calling them is adding fuel to a fire. You're assuming they forgot you and/or didn't let you read for whatever reason. If you call, be prepared to hear something like, "Yes, we know you exist, we only could bring in ten people and unfortunately we didn't feel that you were as strong for this as other people we represent." You are making the agent look stupid and you'll really need to trust that they will bring you in every time they think your right for a part.

The Recording Booth(s) at Your Agency

The agency has recording booth(s) set up. They have been paid for by the agency and are there for the talent to audition for copy that comes in to the office. There may be only one booth or there may be more, it depends on the size of the agency and the budget they have to build one. Recording studios take money to set up. There needs to be a room large enough to hold the recording equipment and another room for the actual voice-over talent to do their work. These two rooms are separated by glass, so that the talent can still see the casting person. I've also been to talent agency's that have just had one room, with the casting associate in a corner, working with equipment and you at the microphone. There are microphones set up along with headphones. This is the same type of process you will have when you go to an audition at a casting facility. The recording booth has been set up for the talent to make it easier for the ad agency to submit scripts. If your agency does not have a booth (some may not), the copy/scripts will go directly to casting houses or you may be asked to go to the ad agency for the audition.

When will I Go In to Read at the Agency?

You may go in every day of the business week or you may only be called once every few weeks. This depends on how much copy comes into the agency and what your agent thinks you are right for to come in and read.

Your agency will call you when there are scripts available for you to come in and read. They usually call the day before to book you for the following day. Some agencies want you in when they open at 9:00 and may want to be done with the casting process by 1:00. Other agencies may bring people in all day. When they call for you to come in, confirm the time that they give you. If you can't make it at that particular time, let them know. They may have you scheduled for a group read (More than one person on the same spot). They may have a certain order of business, so the time is important. They also may just ask you what time you want to come in. Pick whatever time is convenient. If a script is due in two days, your agent will bring in all the appropriate talent, put everyone on the audition tape and Fed Ex it back to the ad agency.

When you come into the office, someone will hand you copy to look over. You will be called in by groups or singles depending on the spot they are recording.

How Many Demo Tapes Does My Agent Need?

I would make about 100 copies when you are starting out. You will want to send out tapes to ad agencies, especially in the city where you live. You'll also want to send to casting houses and keep some to pass out when you meet people who could potentially hire you.

Give your agent at least fifty copies of your tape. If you use J-Cards for your tapes, along with your name, you'll want to include your agent's name and agency phone number. The J-Card is the cover of your tape and functions like a business card, telling people who you are and how to reach you. It fits inside the cassette box, around your tape. Whenever someone needs to reach you, they will go through your agent. The agency provides a logo to the J-Card operation (check with your local tape duplication house to find out where to have them made), so that your tape will be easily identified with your agency.

Your agent needs the tapes to send out and to keep on hand so that he can send it out on your behalf. When you first sign with your agent, he will do a mass mailing to all potential clients, ad agencies, producers and casting directors. Don't worry if you've already sent the tape out to the same places. It is better for a prospective employer to receive two tapes from you, than none. Your agent knows more producers and production companies than you do; they also know exactly where to send your tape. This doesn't mean you should stop sending your own tape out after you have an agent. Keep sending! Especially to casting houses. Only this time, make sure you indicate your agency representation on the tape. Drop by a few casting houses when you are in the area. Introduce yourself to the casting director and give them the tape. They may say they already have it, but now you've just given them a face to put with the name.

How Do I Market Myself?

You are in business. So, take care of business. Watch your back, and don't share all your secrets in every waiting room. Your biggest competition should always be with yourself, but know that competition from others will always exist. Do what you can to protect yourself and promote yourself.

In the voice-over business, you want people to hear you. In order to get jobs, your voice-over tape needs to get in the right hands of the listeners who hire you for the jobs. Even if you mail to a creative director at an ad agency that has never heard of you, write a catchy note along with your tape. Have interesting J-Cards made so it catches their eye. Maybe you'll get one new person to listen to your tape. They may not hire you today or tomorrow, but you never know what could happen several months from now.

> *Many voice-over artists also teach classes. This not only helps them stay vocally limber but is a great way to be out in the public. As well, several people have business cards and always have their tapes on them ready to hand out. I used to give Christmas baskets to all of my regular clients. Keep a list of every job you do during the year and send them a holiday card. It's a great way for them to remember you even if you only did one radio spot at the beginning of the year. It is a nice gesture and reminds them of what a terrific job you did for them. "Hello, do you have anything for me?" (Don't actually write that in the card, unless you're feeling really confident. Do remind them the spot you did. This doesn't just have to be for holidays. Remembering the people you work with and keeping in touch is a great way to ensure repeat business!*

Keep your demo tapes current. If your tape seems to be outdated (material doesn't apply anymore and the spot sounds old) take off the spot and replace it with a newer one.

If there is another market that you want to infiltrate, tell your agent or take a class in that area. In fact, keep on taking classes. You may not be getting all the auditions you want, but to ensure you are ready when you do get them, why not take a class so you're prepared? There are so many different levels of classes from beginning to working out with the professionals. You can always learn something new.

Keep your auditions sharp. Stay professional. Don't drive your agent nuts with phone calls every day; do your job and keep moving. You may go on forty auditions before you book the job. It's a numbers game! Don't get frustrated. One job leads to two and soon you've more than paid for the price of the demo tape and gas all over town!

How Do I Get An Agent in a Smaller Market (and Do I Really Need One?)

When I started out in Kansas City, I didn't have an agent. I took the demo tape around and dropped it off to all the advertising agencies and independent producers, even the sound studios. I started getting calls from the demo tape. Then I started to get work. It would have been easier for me if I had an agent, but as you know, the one I went to see told me to become a secretary, so I was a little turned off. I had to show him I could get the jobs on my own. A few years later, I did get an agent—the only other one in town at the time. By then, I had done several voice-over jobs and he had copies of my tapes to send out. At that time, there wasn't a recording facility at his office. His office was one room. I got sent out to audition. I was one of about five people in town doing voice-overs. Most of the voice-over people were DJ's for the local radio stations and were hired to do the radio and TV spots. I kept competitive and I got well known. I didn't join SAG until I booked my first national spot, so all the work I did was non-union. I did enough to finally make a real demo tape, but my homemade tape still got me my first ten jobs. I think as long as you hustle in a small town, you will get work. Having an agent will definitely help you because you may not know any of the casting people in town or who to talk to. Your agent will be able to hook you up with everyone and it's much easier to book the jobs through the agent.

Call your local union office for a list of local agents. If you can't find a voice-over agent in your town, call the commercial agents and ask if they would consider having a voice-over department, featuring you.

When you get the list of voice-over agents in your town, call and find out the name of the agent. Ask the name of the person you are talking to. Drop by. If it's a smaller town, why not show them your face? They may still want you to just drop of the demo tape with the receptionist. Make sure that you get the name of the person you are dropping off the tape to. They will call you. If you haven't heard from them in a few days, call. Ask if you can set up a meeting. Don't forget to include an inquiry letter with your tape that you drop off. Be sure to include the name of the person receiving the tape. A sample letter follows.

Date

Your Name
Address
City, State, Zip
Telephone Number

Their Name
Address
City, State, Zip

Dear Mr. Wonderful (put the person's name here),

Per my conversation with Becky Wilson, I have enclosed my commercial demo tape. I am currently seeking representation and would love to set up a meeting with you at your earliest convenience. I look forward to speaking with you.

Happy listening!

Sincerely,
(Your name here)

If you have done some voice-over work and you want to mention it in the letter, add it in: "I am the voice of Mr. Potato Chip Diner, Rex's Hamburger Haven and Topsy Tipsy Ice Cream in Shawnee."

This will give Mr. Wonderful an idea of what you do and what kind of spots you've done. If you have done these voice-overs, make sure to put them on the front of your tape. Mix them in with the fakes. If your tape is all fakes, don't supply the information. When you get the meeting and the question comes up, then you can say it is self produced. Your prospective agent may not like the tape and may ask you to get a new demo tape done before they take you on. They will recommend a good sound engineer in town where you can mix a new tape. They may take you on with the tape as is. When you go into the meeting, be upbeat and positive. Talk about any jobs you've done, casting directors and ad agencies that already know you and classes you've taken. If you have no experience at all, that's okay. Let the agent listen to the tape and be the judge. They may send you to a class or give you your walking papers. If they feel you aren't ready for an agent just yet, don't worry. Call the local colleges and try to get some voice-over or narration work for free. Take another class. Practice with more copy. Call local production houses and see if you can get hired for some more non-union work. Maybe one of the jobs you did before, will hire you again for a spot. Don't get discouraged. Everything happens in steps. Just because this agent doesn't take you on, doesn't mean you aren't good. You just may need more practice and someone to give you a chance. Thank them and ask for any suggestions they might have to help you. Suggestions are good. They get you to the next step.

AN INTERVIEW WITH . . .
JEFF DANIS, Voice-over Agent and Department Head, Commercials/Voice-overs, International Creative Management (ICM)

You started in the advertising business?
Yes. I was with an ad agency in New York City for ten years. I did everything from head of casting, talent to payments. Then I worked at J. Michael Bloom as an agent, took a year off to be a casting director and then came to Los Angeles to start the voice-over department at ICM.

Why did you want to go into voice-overs?
I knew they were the thing of the future. I knew that the money potential for talent and agents was big. As a voice-over agent, you have more control of someone's career. There is more longevity in a voice-over actor's career than on camera commercials.

What do you look for in a voice-over client?
Earning potential, unique voice quality, good acting ability. Also, I think very important is a comfortable persona. The ability to read a script is very important. Many actors have trouble with the commercial rhythm. Some stage actors tend to be to broad with the copy, while some film actors tend to be to intimate. There is a definite rhythm to the read. Actors should watch TV commercials and listen to the radio. Ninety-nine percent of the time, the obvious commercial read books the job. All commercial (TV) reads, should fit these ideals; Give it warmth! Give it a commercial read. Most of the time, that will get you the spot or get you close. Voices may sound different, but there is still a definite rhythm to the read. The way a sentence ends. The tone of the voice. Also, timings are very important. Timing has to be there.

How do you differentiate your client list from one another?
Everyone has something different. It is very important to know your clients. I keep a roster in my head. If a producer calls, I know in that minute that I can go through my list and be able to tell them who can do what kind of read. It's very important to know my clients, to know exactly what they are capable of. A lot of producers count on me to help in the casting process. They can call me up and say, "I need a couple for this spot. Woman should be sardonic, man should be nerdy." I can cast that spot in a matter of minutes and know that my clients will be at that job!

What is your suggestion when we come in to read?
When you come in, you should make sure that your read is the best that it can be. Technically your voice should be present on the mike. Make sure that the headphones are up, make sure that you are centered to the mike. We have a digital system. That makes the difference. When the client gets the DAT (Digital Audio Tape), it is very clear. We want the client to be able to hear your voice. I, as your agent, need to be able to showcase you the best way I can. When you go in to read, the very first and very last question that you should ask is; "What am I saying?": If you cannot answer that question, then your read is not the best that it can be. You need to know what you are talking about. The interpretation of the read is very important. A lot of people may read for a job, but the interpretation, the acting, is what gets you the job. Convention is out. They want unique personalities now. They want the copy to come alive, your unique personality to come through.

How many clients do you put on an audition tape?
It depends on the copy. I will stick as many people on a tape that I think are realistically capable of booking that job. It may be anywhere from five to fifteen people. You have to remember that we may or may not be the only ones in town getting the copy. Sometimes with large campaigns, it may go to us, a few more agencies that each put ten or so people on and may also go to Chicago and New York. Sometimes more than one hundred people can be up for the same job!

What do you expect from the voice talent?
I expect them to make the voice-overs a priority. I have one client that has a great voice, but just doesn't book the reads. I have faith in him because I know that he will work. I continue to work with them. Practicing reading is important.

I think it's a great workout just coming into the booth, even if you're not booking. It gives you a chance to read copy, hear what's "in" out there in TV land, and get the rhythm down.
Absolutely. The truth is, a great read (a TV commercial read) can be learned. It is more important to know how to act than to have specific voice quality.

What does it take to make it in this business as a voice-over talent?
Opportunity and ability. Rhythm is everything. Unique personality. I've heard some great voices, but they didn't have any character in their voice. The best reads are the actors who understand what they are saying. Commercials have a simple message "Buy This Product!"

What is the difference between a voice agent and an on-camera commercial agent?
An on-camera agent will have many more clients. Clients can easily become over-exposed. Ad agencies like to see different faces. An actor can be on two or three commercials and they burn out. A voice-over talent can do a lot more work. The agent and talent can make a lot more money over a longer period of time. The voice can work for many years. Much more longevity and potential more often. I also have more control with my clients than if I were an on-camera agent. I can cast the spot and send work my clients way a lot easier than on-camera agents can. I have a lot more opportunity for work for my clients; Radio, TV, Looping, Animation, Non-Broadcast, Industrials, Promos and CD-ROM's.

Let's end this with a bottom line. Have one?
The talent has to be A list. All the good intention that an agent has is only as powerful as the talent is. On that same note, as talented as the talent is, they are powerless without a great agent behind them!

CHAPTER 10

• • •

THE COMMERCIAL AUDITION

• • •

> *I got called for an audition in the valley (forty-five minutes from where I was working as an assistant at a talent agency) and I had to lie to my boss to get there. It was for a campaign for a company called HomeBase. They had seen everyone in town from Julie Kavner (Marge on The Simpsons) to many other stars. I thought that it was the worst audition I had ever done. I went in, and basically "threw the read away." I called my agent and told him that it was the worst audition I had done. Cut to: I booked the campaign for the next three years and that job led to many others and creating an entire new genre for women voice-over actresses. The moral: Trust your gut, do the best job you can do and LET IT GO!"*

Congratulations! You've finally got one. And it may have taken awhile, too. But you're here. So if you've got an audition, you will need to know what to do. Chances are, your first audition isn't through an agent. It was through the work that you did up until this point. Classes, contacts, non-union projects, etc. Whatever it was, you got it!

Don't let the audition scare you. Don't drive yourself or the casting director crazy. It's only one audition and each one you should treat just as an opportunity. There will always be another audition around the corner. You need to be prepared, and do your best. There are so many people and only so many auditions, so really the only thing that you can do is to do the best job that you can, and cross your fingers. One will come along that you will book.

The casting director will tell you if the commercial is radio, TV, animation, national, local, regional or cable. The copy will have the name of the advertising agency on it and you will know if it's radio or TV copy by the way it is written. (TV will have the audio = voice on the right side of the paper and the video = visual on the left side of the paper. Radio will be set up in paragraph form as to be read easily as a commercial). Put the same amount of professionalism into all of your work. You may let the casting director know that it's your first audition, but don't make a big deal out of it. Make sure that you get to the audition in time to read over the copy and have the way that you'd like to read it down. When you go into read, you want to be as professional and you can be. It always helps to act like you know what you're doing, even if you don't. You will learn, with a little help from this book, as you go.

How Do I Dress?

Any way that you want. Remember, you are being heard, not seen. Even if you meet with the client, you are being considered for the voice not the face. You can, however, choose to represent yourself however you would like. They really don't care if you show up in pajamas. The one thing I would say is that if you are trying to do on-camera work too, try to always look your best. I love going out in workout clothes, but when I know that I'm going to a session or a studio, I'll try to get a little dressed up. You never know if they may think you would be right for the on-camera part as well, or the on-camera for another commercial they are shooting. So, dress the way you want to represent yourself. Obviously it's a little difficult to read copy in a grass skirt or fur coat. You will want a little room to breathe and move. Other than that, part of the fun is wearing jeans when everyone else has to wear a suit. I sometimes feel like voice-over artists are the group in high school who always got in trouble and never grew up. Except that we're making lots of money!

How Do I Prepare for the Audition?

The only option that you have is to get to the audition early— twenty minutes or so—and read the copy over. You can ask your agent if you can pick it up a day before, but usually you won't be called for the audition until last minute. They audition and cast fast. Your preparation comes in reading and interpreting the copy, the more that you read and audition. You will learn over time to read the copy and interpret it. Ask a friend if you can read the copy to them to see if it sounds real or not. Play around with the words and inflection. When you go into read, you may get to read more than once so have a few options and attitudes.

Who Will I Be Dealing With at the Audition?

A casting director will come to get you in the order of your call time, and will be the one who will work with you on the reads. They will record you and let you listen back. If you don't get to listen back and want to, ask. If they have time, they will play the take(s) back. At that time, you will get to hear what you did and make the appropriate changes. When you're done reading, leave the copy, thank the casting director and walk out of the room. (If you want copy, take it from the sign in area. There will be a separate piece of copy in the booth for you to read, but do not take that out. It has been placed there by the casting director. You may run into other voice-over artists that will be reading the same copy. Readings are usually scheduled pretty close together. You cannot go into the room and hear what someone else has done, nor can you ask to hear your read way after the fact. The casting director has already edited your read the way they want it and is on to the next audition. They will then send those completed takes from all the talent to the ad agency for them to choose the voice they want.

How Do I Make the Casting Director or Ad Executive Remember Me?

Read well. Be polite, nice and professional. Make sure that your read is professional and in the time they are looking for. The time isn't always important, but if you want to know what time you read a spot in, ask. They will tell you. Always be as quick and professional. Don't waste their time; they have many people to see. If you have a current demo tape that they don't have, leave it. Finish your audition, and then leave. This is the best you can do.

You will get a call for the audition from your agent, client, friend, networking, producer, or a call that you made setting up a time to go into the audition. The casting house or ad agency will either call telling your agent that they want to see you for a read. This audition came either from listening to your tape that you or your agent sent over, or because your agent convinced them you would be perfect for the job.

The casting house and agent will give you a precise time for the audition. Example: 10:35 a.m., 4:50 p.m., etc. Auditions are scheduled in regular intervals: every ten or fifteen minutes. You will be booked for a certain time. They will not ask if you are available. It is up to you to make yourself available.

If it is absolutely impossible to make the audition, let the person know (your agent, casting house, etc.) when you call to confirm the audition. If possible, they will try to reschedule to fit you in. It is important to be available and be prompt. You often get calls the day before or that morning for auditions at the times they have open. They try to schedule according to their day and their session, not yours.

Be Available

Casting directors and agents do not like to take time with people who are changing appointments all the time; they are too busy. You need to change your schedule accordingly. Often, they will be running behind, but you should be on time. They may have you reading in groups and if you're late, you will miss the chance to read. You may be re-grouped in a later group, but don't count on it. They schedule according to type and age, and they may have more than one audition going on at the same time, many casting directors reading different pieces of copy.

No Advance Copy

Unlike other acting jobs, copy is not available beforehand to be faxed, mailed or delivered. You can't pick it up or take it home to study. The voice-over audition process does not work this way. The copy is available only at the audition session. You have to learn how to be spontaneous and prepared quickly. If you feel insecure and shaky, get to the audition early, find the copy you are reading for (don't sign in if you're early and want to study it) and go to another room or outside, and study it. Do what you can to be ready. Once you are in the booth, you will only be in there for five to ten minutes, so you need to be ready to read.

Sign In and Wait

Once you've gotten the copy, the room either will have a sign-in sheet (mandatory for all Screen Actors Guild jobs) or you will see the copy in the room that you enter into. There may be no one at the audition at that time and there may be several. Auditions run closely together. Several voice-over artists will be there from many different agencies and you will be reading against them. Also, you may be auditioning for something that will need five others—a group read. You may know these people or you may not. You've been paired up beforehand by the casting director. You will not know they are your partners until the casting director comes out and tells you. At that time, you can read with your partners if you want to. Ask them if they want to practice. If they don't, don't get discouraged. A lot of people have been in the business for a long time and don't feel the need to study their copy beforehand. A lot of times they like to just go in and read it fresh. Sit and wait until you're called. Sometimes this can be a long process and you may have to wait awhile. If you've been waiting over a half an hour and you need to leave, tell the casting director. At that point they will tell you they are behind or will try to get you in. There is a mandatory one-hour time limit for waiting periods. If you have to wait longer than an hour, the union fines the casting house and they have to pay you a fee. (See "The Unions," Chapter 16).

PREPARE YOURSELF

A voice-over waiting room can be one big party. Remember you are dealing with actors and usually funny ones at that. They all have a story to tell. The feel of the waiting room can vary with the time of day and the amount of copy. If you want to ensure peace and quiet, you'll have to go to another room or move outside. Some people look at the copy once or twice and go in. Others spend ten minutes or so underlining words they want to emphasize, doing arrows for the way they want to end on words up or down. Use any method that works for you to give the best read that you can.

SCRATCH TRACKS AND TIMING

The copy may be television or radio copy. If it's radio, there will be no visual on the copy. The copy is written differently (refer to the sample copy for TV and radio in Appendix A). Take note of what they are selling and how. In television, they will show you the visual (always to the left of the page) and the audio (to the right of the page). Sometimes in television, it will be important to follow the exact timing of the spot. There may be a scratch track (an unfinished version of the commercial) to follow along with once you go into the booth. If one is available, the casting director will let you know at the time of the read. The casting director will play the commercial for you and then you will read. You will need to follow along while you read your copy. The casting director will then play the spot for you on the television. You will watch it and then do your read. On the scratch track, you will hear a voice (usually the writer or producer of the spot) reading the copy. Do not get confused by the voice. And don't copy it. The person reading isn't a voice-over actor, so you should do the read the way you've been instructed to.

The casting director will play the commercial a few times for you to get a feel for it. Take mental notes (or write them down on the copy): the places to take beats, places to go faster, which words are spoken at which visual in the commercial. The ad agency will want a voice that can also be set up to match the timings and visuals of the spot. Of course you will re-do your read when you go in for the session if you book it, but if they have the commercial partially completed, they like to get a feel for how it will sound with your voice. You will not be able to record your voice while the commercial is playing. The scratch track is merely an aid to help you better prepare for your read.

OK, Now Throw It Away

If you put too much emphasis into the read, it won't come across as real and natural and you want to stay real so, no matter how much information you get, once you get it, throw it away. By this I mean, you don't want to sound like a robot when you read. Period here, sigh there, go up on a word there. Make sure that you are sounding real and telling a story. Make sure that you sound like a real person and not an actor trying to read copy. If you put too much emphasis on how you read instead of what you read, your words will sound pushed and fake.

It's Your Turn

When it's your turn, go into the appropriate booth to read. If there are headphones available and you want to use them, pick them up and adjust them to your head. Some casting facilities do not have headphones. In this case, place your copy at fit your eye level and give them a level. The difference with not using headphones, is that you will not be able to hear how you sound while you are reading. Using or not using headphones, if they are available, is a personal preference. If they do have headphones, adjust them to your head by the tightening and loosening level. There will also be a L for Left and a R for right. If they provide headphones, but you feel you read better without them then don't use them. You are not forced to put them on.

The casting director will speak to you from a "talk back microphone." This microphone allows the people outside the recording book to communicate with you. The casting director will ask for a level. Read a portion of the copy in the same level that you will record. After the casting director has done the technical aspect of setting levels, you are ready to read. Now is the time to ask any questions you may have. If you don't understand a word or phrase, are confused by what the ad agency is looking for in terms of voice quality or character, if you are concerned about the pace, ask! They will tell you whatever you want to know. If the copy does not say what the timing is and you need to know, ask that too. Learning to get reads in the proper period of time, helps book the job. If the ad agency hears fifteen reads for a thirty second spot and you were the only one to read it thirty seconds, they may go with you. They know that you can get the read done in time. Most casting directors will not let you go much over the time, but are more concerned with getting a nice read for them to put on the audition tape.

The Read

Should you sit? Or stand? This is up to you. Most casting houses provide a chair. You may want to stand. Standing allows you to more freely move your body and create characters. The casting director will ask you to "slate your name" and begin. Slating is just stating your name and the name of your agent or agency, if you have one. You will begin Take Number One.

If you mess up, they will stop the recording and begin again. You may only read one to three times, depending if the casting director is getting what they want. Read it as many times as they ask. Don't waste the casting director's time with a lot of silly questions. Don't ask to read the copy again, unless you really feel that you can do it much differently. The casting person will tell you what they want, what they didn't get and if you need to do it again. If they don't like the way you are reading something, they may stop you and have you start over.

A Few Do's and Don'ts

- DO make sure that you felt you did the best job you could and pat yourself on the back.
- DO make sure that you felt natural and confident and that you did the kind of read you set out to do.
- DO make sure that if you heard a weird background noise while you were reading and being taped, or if you flubbed a line, tell them. They will let you do the take over.
- DO thank them for having you come in to read. Casting people spend a lot of their time organizing lists of who to bring in. They narrow it down from quite a few people so the fact that they thought of you means they like you and think you have a chance of booking the job.
- DO leave them a current demo tape. You can hand it to them, drop it off if you see an office around or mail it to them.

- DO leave quietly and quickly. Standing around and gabbing may give them the impression that you have no other auditions (let them think you're busy and working) and may distract from people getting ready to audition.
- DO forget about it and head to your next audition.
- DO keep going on with the classes and one will come your way.

- DON'T ask them when they will know if you have the job. They don't know. When they put the audition on tape, they may call the agent directly to book the talent. The casting director will then get a payment for booking out of their casting session. This is paid from the ad agency.
- DON'T ask them if you can call later to find out how you did. Ask them at the time of the audition.
- DON'T ask them to critique you. You can ask your agent later to call them.
- DON'T tell them your life story, or ask to come in again. They will call you or your agent.
- DON'T ask for advice. The audition is not the time or place. They are busy. If you want to ask advice, ask them if you can stop by sometime in the afternoon or a slow period and get some advice for five minutes. I'm sure they will accommodate you or send you in the right direction.
- DON'T call your agent to see if you got a call back. They will call you.

The casting director will smoothly move you through the audition. They may ask for a few different types of reads. The first they may want warm and intimate and the second read they may ask for fun and conversational. They may send both takes to the agency.

They will "playback" the audition for you. This means that they will let you listen to what you have just done in order to make changes or move on to another read. Take this opportunity to listen to the playback and analyze your work. They may playback only one take if they are short on time. Sometimes, they won't play a take back at all. You have to trust that you got the read. One of the best compliments you can get is having them be happy with your read, record it, say thank you and move on. They may have you do two takes for a couple of reasons. They may want you to do it the second way differently: more laid back, more warmth. It could be a number of reasons. They may let you choose how you want to do it a second way. Most times, they will want the first take to reflect what they and the ad agency are looking for.

If you want to get a little crazy or off base with the second read, ask the casting director if that would be all right. Follow your instinct. If you feel something should be read a certain way and you didn't do that, ask to do a take that way. Don't go too overboard, though. The casting director has a lot of people to see and voices to record.

You will not be allowed to take a copy of the audition with you. It has been recorded on a cassette that holds all the auditions.

IMPROVISING

This is a touchy area that is sometimes encouraged and sometimes not. Many voice-over actors will improvise. The safest answer I can give to that question is, if you feel it helps, take the risk, but I'm also a big believer in improvising within the lines that are written. This means following the script but romancing certain words more, adding sounds that are natural to the character and playing with copy more. That doesn't mean changing the word "house" to "trailer." The writer has written the spot for a specific reason. We are there to get the words across to the audience the way they want it said. There is more room for improvisation in radio. If you are reading for a "wild and crazy guy" and you are supposed to "have fun with it", then go for it a little. Just be prepared to pull back for your next take. The casting director will tell you if it's too much.

QUESTIONS TO ASK YOURSELF BEFORE YOU READ

Who am I talking to?
Is the commercial for beer or perfume? Is it Bud Lite or Heineken? How about the perfume: Love's BabySoft or Chanel? Finding out your demographic and age group of the commercial helps in discovering who you are talking to and how to say it.

What am I saying?
Read the commercial. Read it again. Understand what the copy says. How is the product being sold? Is the commercial funny? Sad? Does it subtly push you into buying their product, or boldly? Get what kind of story or message the commercial is pushing. Every piece of copy tells a story in their own way, even if it's badly written.

What kind of a message am I trying to convey?
Am I trying to scare teenagers? Am I trying to teach responsibility to drivers? Do I want someone to read a paper more, buy my toilet paper because it's softer? Am I trying to open your eyes to the beauty of a particular brand of contact lenses? The words, my voice and image (if it's for TV), will sell the product.

What is the "mood" or "attitude" of the spot?
The mood and attitude are the style or feeling that you get when you read the spot.

What is the description telling me in terms of how to read the spot?
The description in the copy or the casting director's instructions will tell you what they are looking for, what the attitude is. Read the copy accordingly.

How do I find the rhythm in a spot?
Commonly, if you just read the copy, it will have a natural rhythm. You need to find it. If you put too much effort in, it will be lost. If you take the time to just read it as if you are reading to someone, the meaning will come out far more clearly.

Read the sample copy in Appendix A. Pay attention to the direction. Read the copy. Try different reads. Time yourself. Record it and play it back. Does it sound like a real person speaking or does it sound forced? Would you buy the product if you heard it on the air? Do you think that people would consider it to be a well done spot? The writer has intended you, as the voice-over artist, to be able to convey the story of the copy. When you are doing a voice-over, you are telling a story. Make sure that you are paying much more attention to what you are saying instead of how you are saying it. If you pay too much attention to your "voice," you will lose the feel of the spot.

CALLBACKS
Callbacks are not as common in voice-overs as in on-camera. Usually, the client will listen to your audition tape once and hire you (or not hire you) for the job. If you are called back, you will be asked to come and read again as early as the next day. You also may be called the next week or a month later. It all depends on when they are planning to record the commercial.

If the agency hasn't decided on a voice or if they haven't yet heard what they're looking for, they may call you in again. You will either go to the ad agency or back to the casting house to read. This means that they like you but have narrowed it down to a few people. They could be deciding between using a man or a woman; or between several types. Be on time, study the copy and do the same thing that you did in the audition. Treat this audition as you did the first audition for this product. They may give you different direction. Follow what they say and read the copy again.

Sometimes, commercials are scrapped all together. Perhaps nothing worked: the copy, the concept, the voices, etc. The client simply might not like the commercial that the ad agency has written. They may drop their campaign altogether, or hire a different ad agency. There's a lot more involved than just your voice. The callback generally means that you are in the running and being considered for the job.

DEMOS

If you are hired for the job, but the client and ad agency aren't completely sold on your voice or the idea for the spot, they will ask to do a demo. The process may go from audition, to callback to demo to airing the spot. This sounds like a long process. Usually, you will audition and then be called by your agent to tell you that you booked the job.

A demo is the non-air version of the spot, meaning it is a spot that they are NOT planning to air on TV or radio. They may use it to test within their company or ad agency; or, they may let a group of recruited "civilians" (people not in the business) listen/watch and voice their reactions. Depending on the response from the test, the agency will decide whether or not to air the spot(s). If the decision is yes, you will be upgraded from a demo session rate to a regular session rate which is higher.

If this is a non-union job, all jobs are negotiated according to the terms that you and your producer, writer, director agree upon. If you want the experience, work for less money. A non-union, non-air demo is still worth doing if you need the tape. Most likely, they are doing the demo for the same reason that an ad agency would do: to see the response. You can request the tape from a non-union, demo job and if the commercial airs, you can negotiate a further fee based on the fact that it aired. Non-union commercials usually only pay a single fee. Budgets are small and there are no residuals. (See "The Unions" Chapter 16.)

Demo jobs are very normal. The more people involved in an ad agency for a spot, the more creative minds there are. This means more discussion and less agreement on the spot. They may not even know if they want to go male or female. The demo allows all parties involved to pull you into a recording studio and use you for as long as one to one and one-half hours. This is the time allowed, per Guild rules, for one session to run. If they use you longer than that, they will need to pay you the demo rate again. Usually, they will bring you in and have you read the copy a number of ways. They will not let you know right then if you booked the spot. They are still seeing other people and discussing the final outcome with the client.

I did a campaign for NESTLE SENSATIONS. I had auditioned originally, got called back and went to the ad agency. After the callback, they called my agent and hired me for a demo. I went back to the ad agency (they had their own recording facility. As businesses are becoming advanced, especially larger advertising agencies, they have built their own recording studios). I did four spots, several different ways. I had my agent call the ad agency several months later to see if they would be airing. The ad agency said that they were still studying the spots and weren't really sure if they would ever play. I still have not heard them on the air and I'm not sure if they will ever come out. I got a one time demo fee and that was it. If they air, I will be paid an upgrade and will begin seeing residuals every time they air.

DEMOS FOR ANIMATION, LOOPING, NARRATION AND PROMOS

The process is basically the same for these categories as it is for commercials. Sometimes a demo is a chance for them to hear you in their studio with actual visuals. These things may not have been at the original read, but this doesn't mean that they got the professional sound and final read they were looking for in the actual session, so they will book a session with you and have you come back in to read. You will be paid for a demo as well as an additional promo fee. All sessions for union jobs are an initial payment of scale just to bring you in. After that, depending on the job; Looping, Animation, Narration, Promo, Audio Books, TV or Radio, plays the role in defining how much you will be paid per union rules.

As for animation, you may be pulled in to read your character(s) with other actors who are being considered for the part. Also, the animated film or TV show, may not have been sold. The director may want to lay down the entire episode and see if he/she can sell it. You will be paid according to your time and the demo rate. You may also be called in to do a slightly different version of what you did at your callback if they still feel that you didn't quite get the read. They will direct you and work with you until they get what they want. Animated sessions are longer and work at a different pace than commercials. They may record you alone, playing back the other person's read that you will be reacting to. Other times, you will have to use your imagination and pretend to react to another voice that hasn't been recorded yet. A session can last all day.

The process is the same for narration, looping and recording audio books. You will meet with the writers, directors, producers, sound engineers and record whatever copy they give you. If the book is sold, if they like your voice, if any number of reasons point to hiring you, then you will then be called back in to do the real session. You will have done a demo of a small portion of the job. A narration job can sometimes be several pages. Looping an entire movie can take days. Recording audio books is a very long process so they will only record part for the demo. The producers will make their decision from there.

What's Next?

OK, so now you've done it—you've completed the audition. Now what? Now forget about it. Don't make calls all around. What you can do is:

- Write down the name of the ad agency and send them a current tape.
- Keep the copy if you want for future use for your own benefit.
- Keep a file with the ad agencies for holiday cards, mass mailings, etc.

This is all smart business, and will help you get future jobs. As for this one? Forget about it.

All you can do now is wait. Go on another audition and another. It's all a numbers game. You may book your first job or you may not book anything until the 100th audition. Each one leads to the next one. You will get better each time you audition. Keep at it, and have fun. Somewhere along the way, you'll book a job. By then, you'll be on five auditions, three sessions and a callback, and you'll have to check your schedule.

CHAPTER 11

• • •
OTHER AUDITIONS
• • •

ANIMATION

The animation audition follows the same process as regular commercials. Though you will probably go to Disney, Warner Bros. or the production facility that is doing that particular animated series rather than an independent recording studio. You will enter a waiting room and sign in. You will know which character you are reading for because your agent will have told you when he called you with the audition. For an animated audition, there will be the copy and often a sketch and description of the character. The picture is a great tool for deciding what kind of voice to try. They aren't always sure what they are looking for, just like in regular commercials. You may see a drawing of an elephant wearing boxer shorts and have to come up with your own version of how he or she would sound. There are several different descriptions that they may give you (either with thedescription and picture or told to you by your agent). They may say, "Flippo is slow but not dumb, pensive yet determined. He's a tough rebellious teenager with a heart of gold. " This is very common for an audition. Your job is to interpret how you think Flippo will sound. You will probably read a couple of times once you go in the audition room. The audition room is just a studio set up with a microphone and a sound engineer or the casting director on the other side. They may ask to hear a bit of what you are going to do. At that time, if you're unsure about what angle to take, ask.

A casting director is more than happy to say, "we're looking more for a higher pitched teenager" or "We see Flippo as slow and maybe a New York accent." Any of these can be interpreted any number of ways. The only job that you have as the voice-over actor is to be professional and have fun in the audition. Make it real for yourself. In animation, it is very important to make the character come to life. You have to bring the written words to life. You will not have a television set up with your character up there to read along. The only visual you will have is the picture. Sometimes the animator will be in the audition and other times, the animated show isn't even close to completion. Maybe all the animators have at this point are character pictures and a storyline. They may be waiting for the voice-over actors to fill the body of the characters they've drawn before they come up with an entire show. Once they hear voices they like and feel fit the character they've imagined, the process can be completed. You may be called in to read for more than one character. This is completely normal. Just find a change in your voice and do different characters to fit what you think the animated characters would sound like. You may be able to pick up the sides or copy beforehand so that you can study. Ask your agent or go by the studio to pick up the sides. Take them home if you want.

Sometimes for an animated movie or TV series, there will be a completed script for you to read. It will give you a full view of what the story line is and how your character develops throughout the show. In an animated audition, you'll want to make sure and give the character you're reading for lots of color and depth. Don't read for the sake of getting the words out. If "Flippo" is falling over the side of a cliff only to land on a safe cloud, incorporate that into your read. Make sure that you sound like "Flippo" falling off of the side of a cliff (exasperated noises and all) only to be comforted by the cushioning of a feather filled cloud (Ahh!) The character must feel life. Don't fret if you don't get the job. So many people read for each part, and you won't know what someone else did. When the show comes out, then you see who booked your part and why. Sometimes they are looking for something very specific and they only know it after you read. Other times, they may have thought they were going one way and completely switched. The best thing that you can do is just make sure you are getting out there to read for everything you can. Taking that animation class and having an up to date animation tape is the key to successfully staying ahead of the game. One of these days, it will all pay off.

Looping

There really are not looping auditions. You will need to find the loop group(s) in your area and call. Find out if they will accept your tape. Call post production facilities and find out how you can be a part of their stable of loopers. Do they use a specific loop group or do they accept submissions? Can you get in with them when they need someone to loop their next project? Find out if any of the loop groups offer classes. Take the class.

Dubbing

Don't confuse looping with dubbing. Are you thinking "When she says looping, does she mean mimicking the voice and matching it to the screen?" No. That is dubbing. Dubbing is anything that you have to record over what has been there. You specifically have to match the line "Wait until morning," to the voice saying it on screen. Many dubbing jobs are from another language. If you are fluent in any foreign language, this may be a perfect career for you. You will go into a studio where a chair and monitor will be set up. The copy is in front of you in the language you need to dub it in. The scene will come on the screen in the language it was recorded. You will then match the tonality of the voice you are hearing (sounding as much like this person as possible) and say the words to match the mouth movement. Dubbing requires lots of patience and talent.

Call dubbing houses to find out about dropping your tape off and auditioning. Call a specific dubbing house in your area that specializes in a dialect you know or, if you're especially flent in French, you will probably do well with French films that need to be dubbed into English. Foreign voice-over actors work all the time. They dub shows like *Friends* and *ER*, they also dub movies of the week and feature films.

Narration/Promo

You will be called by your agent and you will go to the appropriate studio or production facility. These studios and production facilities have their own casting directors as opposed to casting houses hired for a day to bring in talent. You sign in, get your copy and wait for them to call you. Same setup. Microphone, casting director, headphones. You will read all or some of the copy depending on what they want you to read and you will leave. They may ask you to read again or slower, deeper, faster, more energetic. There may be a TV monitor in front of you if they have the commercial up. You will read to the actual commercial after a series of three beeps that will lead you in (just as when you are doing looping or dubbing, this gives you a cue to start talking along with the visual). They will record your take and that is all. For narration, you will generally have longer copy. You most likely will be narrating the entire commercial or industrial. They want to hear a smooth, consistent read that matches the product they are selling.

The copy will have direction with the kind of voice and attitude they are looking for. You've most likely been called in because they have a copy of your demo tape that your agent has sent them, so they have a pretty good idea of the quality of your voice. They aren't looking for a zany character read. Depending on the product, they will want a voice that will carry them nicely through the selling of their product. It may be a sweet, high pitched voice or a low, deep throated sell. Deep men's voices often come to mind when thinking about narration jobs, but not always. Narrators come in all sounds depending on the sell. Promo voices ("Tonight on CBS"), will generally be men, but from time to time you do hear women.

I'm known in the promo world for a more fun, energetic read and depending on the TV show, they will call me in to audition for that type of read. As you listen and watch TV, notice how certain nights of TV will have a voice quality to match the programming, depending upon if it's serious or funny. Steve Mackel, who is the voice of NBC lineup Thursday nights, is energetic and zany. The current voice for NBC Thursday night shows are even lighter and zanier to attract a younger crowd.

When you watch *Dateline*, notice the voice that promotes the show. It's a very deep, authoritative voice that suits the age group and seriousness of the show. Older, deeper, reassuring, professional sounding voices are used. It matches the demographic of the audience they are selling to. It wouldn't fit to have a spacey, teenage girl saying, "Tonight on *Dateline*, War in Bosnia." You wouldn't take it seriously, would you?

Promos are very serious business. For the few words that you say, you are representing an entire demographic. Learning to audition well for promos takes practice. (I don't know of any promo classes, but if your voice fits in to voices you hear on TV and the radio, work on those things in class. Make a specific demo tape and send it to the studios. You want to be able to be called. Ask your agent if they have specific promo department and how you can advance your career in this area.)

STRATEGIES FOR SURVIVING YOUR DAY IN VOICE-OVERS!

Keep it fresh.

Read every voice-over audition as if it's your first.

Do the best you can for that particular spot, then forget about it.

Don't worry about "awful" reads. Remember how many times you thought (and were told) you were "wonderful" and still didn't get the job.

Don't second guess or try to one-up any other auditioner. You'll take away from the power of your own voice.

Improvise where you see fit, but don't let it detract from the read. The copywriter wrote the copy for a reason, no matter how bad it is.

Try new kinds of reads within the same attitude.

If you want to read twice and they let you, do something different!

Let it go after you read.

Watch your (sentence) endings.

Breathe naturally.

If you're not sure how to read something, ask.

Don't get overconfident.

CHAPTER 12

• • •
THE SESSION
• • •

> *I was in a very long session. The company that hired me told my agent that I would only be doing ten tags. In fact, I did twenty. Because I already signed the contract and left as it was being typed, and the contract showed only ten tags, I never got paid for the additional work. Now I always check what I am doing and make sure that I never sign a contract unless it is correct. Call your agent first and tell the producer of the spot. I lost thousands of dollars for that mistake.*

Congratulations! Now it's time to record your spot and get paid. Your agent, or whomever you book the job through, will call you to give you the time and date of the session. Once you are booked for a job, you cannot change your time. The ad agency has gone to great lengths to find a studio available and to make sure you're available. Or, a phone patch (see below) has been arranged for a specific time. Make sure that you are on time! Studios run by hours and the client has booked you for a specific amount of time.

The only thing you need to bring is your voice. Once you arrive, check in with the front desk. Tell the receptionist which job you are there for, the time, and tell them that you are the talent. The receptionist will have a list of all jobs, ad agencies, time booked and which room you are recording in. She will also have the copy if it's available. If the ad agency is not there yet, they will be bring the copy with them. If it's a phone patch, the sound engineer may have your copy. Just ask for it and someone will get it for you to go over. Sit in the waiting area and study.

Contracts

The copy and contract will have been sent to the studio. If there is no contract, tell the producer once you end the session, and call your agency and tell them the number of spots you did. If the job is union, fill out the union papers, which the studio provides and sends to your union. The producer may fax the contract straight to your agent, or they may ask you to fill it out and then fax it.

For non-union work, there will be no paperwork and you will be paid "under the table." You will have negotiated the rate with the producer, advertising agency, director, etc. Generally there is no formal contract.

Recording the Session

There are three basic ways to record the session: Patch (Land or Phone); In Person, In Town; and In Person, Out of Town

Patch (Land or Phone)

For a phone patch, you are in the studio recording the spot, while the producer, client, director and writer are patched in from another studio. For a land patch, the producer, director and writer are in the studio recording the spot, while you are patched in from another studio.

On a patch the producer, client, director and writer, etc., may be in different parts of the country. You were hired in Los Angeles, and the client is in New York while the writer and ad agency may be in Denver. You will conduct the entire session through the headphones with them. The only people physically present in the session will be you and the sound engineer.

The writer and/or producer(sometimes the same person) will direct you through out the session. This is the person whom you will talk to at the beginning and introduce yourself. The sound engineer will set up all the technical parts, headphones, microphone, and will get you set up. Then he will call the client. At that time the session will begin, and they will put you through with the writer. The client may be on the line as well, just listening to the session. They may be in the same state as the ad agency or you may have a conference call.

Patches (land or phone) are being used more frequently these days. The technology of digital phone lines has improved to the point where it doesn't always make sense to fly everyone across the country and record in a sound studio.

☞ *DO NOT TOUCH THE MICROPHONE! This is the sound engineer's job and they don't want anything broken. If you are having problems with the microphone, let the sound engineer know, they will readjust accordingly. Pick up your headphones, but wait until the sound engineer tells you it's okay to put them on. They may be doing some technical things and you will get a tone in your head if you have them on. This is good for a headache for a few days, so wait until they give you the OK.*

During the patch, the director and/or writer will give you directions through your headset. The sound engineer from the recording studio where you are recording your session will give you the take numbers and any technical information. The sound engineer will give you your timings, slate each take and point at you to begin your read. Another sound studio that is calling in may also have a sound engineer on that line taking takes and timings. Follow theinstructions given to you by sound engineer. Usually it will be the engineer in the room with you.

Sometimes, during a patch, they will both be recording and both be slating. So you will have bothsound engineers taking all the timings and slating you for each take. It is up to them what they want to do. Just follow whomever slates you and tells you to. When you are done with each take, the writer/director will tell you each new piece of direction and guide you. At this point, you should be keeping notes on your script and writing down each change as they give it to you. This way, you will remember what you should do for your next read.

I once had a session for Visa where the ad agency was in New York, the client (Visa) was in Chicago and another voice-over talent (my "husband") was in Atlanta, Georgia. How's that for complicated? Here's what happened. I got called by my agent. I went to the booking (session) at 10:00 a.m (1:00 p.m. in New York and Atlanta; noon in Chicago). I arrive and the sound engineer already has everyone on the line in my headphones. The sound engineer hands me the script and I go into the booth. I put on the headphones and say hello. Everyone is there. My "husband" and I say hello and begin to read the copy through for the level (sound check). We begin the session.

DEFINITIONS TO REMEMBER

TIMINGS: The time allowed for you to read within the take. Just because a spot is called a "thirty-second spot," doesn't mean you will read for the entire time. There may be four seconds of music and there may be another voice playing the announcer or another part. You may only have ten seconds to read your part. They will let you know at the session.

SLATE: This means, "Say your name and take number." In an audition, you may say the take number, but in a session, the recording engineer will do it. The slate in a session means the sound engineer calling off the take numbers after reciting the name of the product. This gives the ad agency the chance to pick the certain take that they liked when editing. They may want pieces from take two and take seventeen. This way they have a slate number to refer to.

LEVEL CHECK: The sound engineer will check the loudness of your voice through the microphone as you speak. You will read the copy or script that is in front of you for your session. Read from the top and continue until the sound engineer has adjusted his levels so the spot will come out crisp and clear. Make sure that your headphones are set properly. There are two places to adjust the headphones. Through the sound engineer's equipment and through your own box, which is attached to the headphones next to your microphone. Adjust your headphones so you hear yourself talking and can hear the sound engineer in them, but not so loud as to give yourself a headache, or can't hear anything at all except your own voice. Make sure that it's at a comfortable level for you to read.

HOT: When you hear a buzzing in your headphones or a screeching noise, your headphones are turned up too high. This is the same thing as when the sound engineer says, "Your headphones are too hot." He may also say "You are feeding back," which means that your headphones are on too high and your voice is pushing back into the studio and will not be able to record.

IN PERSON, IN TOWN

If the client and ad agency and you are all in the same town, you will working with them directly. You will still go into the booth and be set up by the sound engineer. You will be introduced to the person who will give you direction. They will guide you through the session. Direction covers everything they want from a read. Once they get the timing they are looking for, they then may dig into getting the type of read they want. They've chosen you because you are the voice that they want, but they will want to "manipulate" and "play" with your voice, until they get the read that they are looking for.

IN PERSON, OUT OF TOWN

The ad agency may choose to fly you in rather than work with the phone patch system. Some agencies don't feel as comfortable with a phone patch. Some clients or agencies feel they can't hear you read as clearly over a phone line as they could if they were right in front of you in the same booth. It's basically the same system—they just will be on a phone and may feel not as in control of directing you as if they were there, in person. An ad agency spends just as much on flying you out as they do for the price of the digital phone patch, so it's up to them. If they fly you, they will cover the flight and give you a per diem, that should cover the cost of a meal and local transportation (the union sets a minimum amount, but depending upon the city you're going to, you may be able o negotiate a higher amount). If this doesn't cover the costs, tell your agent. You should have enough. You will be told where and when to go. You will pick up the itinerary and ticket, unless it's at the gate waiting for you when you check in, and schedule your day accordingly.

On most of these jobs you would fly in and fly out the same day. If you need to go a long distance (across the country, for example) then you will need to say overnight. The company will pay to fly you to your destination, and if they need you for two days, they will pay your hotel expenses and per diem as well as yourusual fee. The session itself is conducted the same way. You are still in a session and working with the people who are there. You will fill out the proper paperwork, save the receipts from the cab fare and meals and give them to the producer. They may have you fill out a form with the information, and you will sign the contract for the job there. It is up to you to make the flight on time and get the studio.

DEMO SESSION

You have booked the job to do a demo. You will be paid a demo rate. If it is non-union, the fee will be whatever you had previously approved. The demo session is considered non-air, meaning that it will not be broadcast. If it is broadcast, you will then be paid a higher rate. The unions keep track of what is aired. If your commercial airs, you will then be paid accordingly. If the ad agency is on top of things, they will send your agent a check when they decide to air the spot. You will go into the session the same way, recording the spot and leaving. This spot may go on to be broadcast. If it does, they will let your agent know or call you at a later date and upgrade your contract to pay you the scale fee. If it is a non-union job, chances are you will just be paid the one-time fee. The demo session is considered to be a trial of the commercial that they have put together to see if they can sell it to the client. The ad agency may be up for the job and they want to use you to sell the spot or they may already have the job and just aren't sure about the particular spot or you as the talent. They may be bringing in a few people for demos.

REGULAR SPOT

For the regular spot, this is just a general term I used for the session. You will just go in and do the copy/script as written, and they will direct you. This is for a broadcast spot and means that it will be going on the air; either television and radio. You will go in and do your session the way you normally would for a session and you will work with the director. They may need to piece together many takes to get the one they want. The final one that they edit and choose will go on the air. At that time, you may ask for a copy of the spot. If they are finished with it, the sound engineer will make you a copy and give it to you. If they are not finished with it, the ad agency will take your home address or the address of your agent and mail you the completed spot on cassette, DAT, 3/4" or 1/2" tape.

☞ *Unless you just want a tape for your own personal listening (or viewing) pleasure, always request a DAT copy. The sound is much clearer than other formats and will transfer better to your reel. Otherwise a 3/4" or 1/2" cassette will do.*

TAGS

If you are called in for the "tag," you will be reading just a portion of the copy—usually, the very last line. When you are booked for the commercial, you may not know you are doing the tag. There may be a narrator, who introduces the story, voice actors who do the body of the spot (i. e., the "meat" of the copy) and then you, who will do the "tag." Just follow the direction, keep your agent informed of any changes, and you'll be fine.

When you are asked to read the tag three times in a row it is called, "wild lining." You will record these lines or phrases without reading from the full copy. This way, if the agency hears a particular tone or mood they like, it will be easier for you to sustain it when reading three rather than reading one at a time. It takes too long to record one at a time. You will be slated alphabetically after each slated number. For example the sound engineer, following however many regular reads you have done, will say "This is take 14 A, B and C."

This means that you will be slated A, B, C and then you record. You will take a breath between each take and continue until you've done all three. The sound engineer may give you the timings between each read so that you will know to get the read in the proper time that the ad agency is looking for. If you are long on a read, you will know to speed up the next one and vice versa. They may ask you to do it again slower, faster or different pacing and tone. You will still be directed. They will air the tag with the regular spot. If you are doing the commercial with other people, you will be set up with them in the room and just do the part when your part is called for in the spot.

PROMOS

If you are called in for a promo, this means that you are called in to read for a television station, radio station, or some type of promotional ad or campaign. You are the voice reminding viewers when a show is coming on or when the news will air. The promo person differs from the tag person, because the promo announcer may read several lines of copy introducing something and the tag person is just stating a product or a line/phrase that makes you remember the product.

Again, if this is a local non-union job, you will have negotiated this beforehand or at the session with the person who hired you for the job. You may be doing a promo for a local news station or radio station. Promos cover a current, very specific, time frame. "Tonight on *Action 4 News*," "Later on *Friends*," "Next Monday on *A Current Affair*."

ANNOUNCER

The announcer's part could be anything from the entire spot if it's all done by the announcer or just a few sentences with other people. The announcer is the one selling the product. You will do the session the same way: either the other talent will be there or you will have been booked separately. If the other voice actors ("Tom" and "Nancy") have already recorded their copy ("talking about Taco Bell while playing tennis"), the client and ad agency will play it for you and you will work from it. You will then record your part separately, and it will be edited in. They may tell you that you have "24 seconds" and that it's a "60 second spot." This means that the other time is used up with Tom and Nancy, music and tennis ball sounds. You will have to get your read in twenty-four seconds. Sometimes, if they can't get the read in the time, they may have to cut copy. If they like the read and they don't want to cut, they may shorten the music track at the top or skip one tennis ball sound effect, or shorten Nancy and Tom's read.

NARRATION

Narration can have several connotations. It can be another name for the announcer. It is also another name for the person speaking on an industrial or animated show. The narrator's voice will be that one who carries you through the show. The narrator is the person who talks to the audience and tells the story. It is a monologue, not a dialogue.

Recording narration is like a regular session. You may or may not be reading to a visual. It depends on if it's a radio or TV spot. If you don't read to the visual, the ad agency hasn't completed the spot(s) yet or they may show you the completed spot but want you to read wild (without the picture). Sometimes the ad agency feels that they will get a better read from you if you read it wild, because you will have fewer constraints. If you are doing narration for an industrial, you will most likely have the visual prompter (TV) set up to read to. For a narration job, you will have more time to read because you will have more copy to read. Narrators can read anywhere from one paragraph to several pages. You will know the length of the job when your agent calls you. If you want the copy ahead of time to go over and if the agent can get it for you ahead of time, they will. Otherwise, you will get the copy when you go to the session. There may or may not be other people reading with you.

ANIMATION

In the animation session, unless you only have a couple of lines, the animation house will deliver the copy to you beforehand. You will show up at the correct address on time. You will most likely be giving the same read to them that you gave in the audition. The director will direct you. If it is a single, you will be alone in the booth. If you are hired for a day along with other actors, you will each be given your own mike and headphones, and you will all work together, each scene. Each scene will be broken down by page, and you will work that way. They still may have you go in and do a wild line, or three in a row, depending on when they playback and what they like.

SINGLES, DOUBLES AND GROUP SESSIONS

If you are called in for a single, this just means that it is you, and only you, in the spot. There may be music or sound effects added in before or after, but you are the only one reading the copy. Now, this does not mean that there will not be a tag person or someone reading the announcer part in the beginning, middle or end. This just means that you are the only "other" voice besides the announcer. You may also just be the sole voice for the entire copy. You may be reading the body of the spot, the tag line and the announcer copy. (Note: You will NOT be paid three times. You are only paid per spot that you do. If you do several parts—announcer, tag and body— you are still only paid the one fee. You are not changing your voice in any way for the other roles, you are the same voice throughout the entire read.

Doubles mean there are two people in the spot. There may also be an announcer, but basically it's you and the other person. You will each have your own mike and headphones if you are reading together. It's also possible that the other person will record in a separate session.

In the group session, you will work with the other actors for the spot. This will include as many actors as needed for the spot you are recording. If the spot requires seven actors, their will be seven actors at the session. In animation, they may double up and use the same actors for several different characters. This is because in animation, it is much easier to disguise your voice. In regular commercials, it would be too easy to detect, unless the reads are so different from one another that the ad agency decides to use you for two completely different characters. Also, if those voices don't come up next to each other in the spot, they are much more likely to use the same person for two voices. As a general rule though, they will pull in all seven actors to fill all seven roles.

There will be individual mikes and headphones set up. You can all choose to use, or not use, headphones, but it's better to all do the same. It's easier to work off of one another if you are all on the same level and able to communicate with or without. If the client is there, you don't have to wear the headphones, they will speak to you by using the talk back mike.

You will be directed together. The engineer will slate and get a level from each of you, and then you will begin. You will read the copy together. The director may have each one of you go back and do a wild line, meaning they want to re-do a particular word or sentence that may be edited in to the final read.

☞ *Once the talk back mike is on, you are "hot." This means you are "live" and everyone can hear what you say. EVERYONE! So, say nice things!*

Radio Spot

If you are doing a radio spot, the copy will be given to you and you will record it. It may be a group read, a double, or a single. There may be music and sound effects, or not. Radio spots air only on radio. You will have other copy if you are doing the TV version of the spot. They may have a music bed underneath the copy or in front of it already edited and you will be reading with that in the background or front or back. They will tell you the time that they need to get the spot in, and you will do your reads.

Television

You will be given the copy which will look similar to the sample copy in Appendix A. You will read the copy according to the times that they ask for. If they have different story boards, which are pictures of the visual, you will read along with the copy, using the storyboards as a model. If there is a scratch track, you will follow along with the picture while you read. They may show you the spot first, then have you go in and read. Sometimes they want you to read along to picture and other times you will just do it cold. It will depend on what the director wants. If you feel it's easier to read to picture, and they can, tell them. They will be happy to oblige. Otherwise they may show you the spot to get a "feel" for what they want from you. Then you will just watch it and record separately. They will edit later.

In all the sessions, the director will playback whichever takes they are interested in. This may involve you doing a number of takes first and then they will let the sound engineer know which take they like. They may have you read again similar to a take they like, but give you a different piece of direction. Each time, like building a house, you will add on, meaning that you will ad different texture and style to the read according to what the director wants. You may also be asked to take off, making less of the character, not pushing the accent or character so much. The director will direct you with the other actors or play for you what the other actor already did. Sometimes, you will not hear another actors read and will have to react off of the director reading the other person's lines. This is where acting comes into play. It is so important to make your work sound and feel real. It's your job to make sure that the listener feels like you, as the character, are really going through what you are saying in the lines.

MISCELLANEOUS

Time Code Clocks

You may or may not have a time code clock to time your reads. A time code clock is a digital clock set up that times your read from the time you begin speaking. The sound engineer stops it when you have finished reading and tells you your timing. You will be told beforehand how much time you have for the spot. If there is no clock, don't worry. Some places have them, others don't.

Microphones

Different studios have different types of microphones, covers, music stands, microphone set ups (where you push volume level). Even lighting and chairs may be different. Some booths have microphones with volume controls for you, others don't. Once you begin to work in your town a lot, you will become familiar with the way the studios work.

Parking

Some studios have valet parking. It depends, again, on parking lot size, studio size and the kind of facility that you are going into. Allow enough time to park and make it to your session with plenty of time to spare.

Script Formatting

Some television commercials usually show the visual on the left hand side of the script and the audio on the other. Animation may have the drawing next to it or may be written in paragraph form. Radio copy may be set up line to line. When you get into the session, confirm with the writer/producer/director whether or not they want you to pay attention to any line breaks. Often, the copy is broken up the way in which they want the pauses and inflections.

Physical Variances at Studios

Studios sets ups vary from one to another. You may be working where you can see the sound engineer and client/ad agents through a glass window. You will always be in another room, where the acoustics are set up for you to record. Depending on the studio, you could be set up in a room where you don't see anyone, but be able to hear them through your headphones. Or, you may see them on a television monitor.

"Avoid spitting on the glass while recording. It grosses people out and makes that sound engineer's job a lot harder."
—Dan Gilvizan, v/o actor

CHAPTER 13

• • •

THE ADVERTISING AGENCY

• • •

In the world of commercials, a client (e. g., Mervyn's Department Store), decides it wants to run a special campaign. It hires an advertising agency. The agency comes up with the concept. Depending on the budget and market that the client wants to hit, this could be a series of regional spots, or a national campaign. When all these decisions are made, then the search for the voice-over person will begin. If you are a well-known voice, sometimes the spot will be created around the idea of using you. Otherwise, you come in much later in the picture.

Often, ad agencies bid against each other to win accounts. This may be where the agency will need you to do a demo. This demo will, hopefully, win them the account. The ad agency is responsible for finding the talent after the job is created.

"Ad agencies are always looking for fresh talent. Never listen to negative input."
—Michael Donovan, v/o animation actor

Michael's first job was for NBC as "Captain N." He put a demo tape together in his house. A friend heard the tape and recommended him for animation. One call led to another and he was on his way!

An Interview with...
JEFF NICOSIA, Copywriter,
TBWA/Chiat/Day Ad Agency In Venice, California

Chiat/Day recently merged with TBWA (famous for their Absolut Vodka ads) and currently is the 15th largest agency in the country, bringing in $3 billion worldwide. Some clients include Nissan, Infinity, Energizer, Sony, Playstation, Apple, ABC and Taco Bell. Currently Jeff is a radio copywriter for ABC television shows.

What does your job entail?
First, I am assigned to an account for the product—the television show. A copywriter (usually just one for radio) is put on the job. Then I spend some time looking at the television show and begin to write. I may do as many as ten re-writes before the script is approved. Here is the level of approval: Account Executive, Account Supervisors, Brand Managers (the Client).

The most important thing to remember is that a copywriter's job is to write the spot. When I'm writing, I think of a voice. Then I sit down and listen to the CD (usually the house CD's of voice-over agencies) and pick voices. A common session may be selecting five or six voices. At that point I call the agencies, fax the copy and either specifically request that client or suggest the certain category and let the agents put their clients on tape and pick the talent from there.

What do you want from the talent you hire?
By the time a script makes it to the air, here are the things that the writer wants from the talent:

Be easy to work with; be on time; don't get an attitude; don't direct the writer (director) and do not re-write the script! By the time that script has gotten into the hands of the talent, we have done our work. We want the voice-over talent to be easy, fast and good! I love finding new talent, but there are so many voice-over people, that you'd better be easy to work with.

What is your number one rule?
Get a pager!

I thought pagers were usually used so agents could find their clients.
Same reason. We may need to find you or we will call your agent at

the last minute and they will call you. A lot of times, especially when it's radio with a very quick deadline, we look for people who can work at the last minute. We need to be able to call the agent, who in turn can call the talent to get to the job at the last hour. Having a pager means you are available and ready. I had to cast a spot a couple of weeks ago at the last minute and the guy wasn't available and we found another guy with a similar voice quality. It led to 30 spots! It was just as easy to keep using the same guy because he was a pleasure to work with and easy to find!

What annoys you most about talent?
Being late! The writer, producer, ad people and sound engineer have all put in their time and money, and are now waiting for you. BE ON TIME!

How do you feel about talent sending notes to the copywriter or little gestures that have to do with the account?
It's nice to get reminders, but don't do overkill.

Is there anything that you have a hard time finding?
"Real people" reads from actors. Most jump into their "announcer" read. Often I get the actor into the studio and then just have to ask simple questions, such as "Where did you drive in from today?" When then start to answer in their "real" voice, I stop them and say, "That's the read I'm looking for." It's conversational. It's real. And, it's hard for actors to do.

Do you use beginners?
I prefer working with professionals. Beginners also "announce" when reading. Often I've cast a spot from a demo and not really known what that person is capable of. Sometimes it's hit or miss. Stage actors are not always the best Voice-over actors. Finding someone with microphone experience is usually the best bet.

Do you work with celebrities?
I recently hired Mary Gross, formerly of *Saturday Night Live*, for a very sweet, ditzy woman read. I loved working with her because she was very easy to work with and fit the spot perfectly. I would definitely hire her again.

Would you ever hire her for another type of read?
It would be interesting to have her read against type, but usually I

write the spot with a particular person or type of person a specific type of voice in mind. I can be persuaded to go a different way if I hear something interesting.

How do you feel about hearing a woman's voice on a casting tape that you specifically asked for men?
It's interesting and I'm not opposed to hearing them. I will admit that the first voice I tend to go for is a man's. Many of the clients are the same way. They are traditionalists and they stick to what sells. Most clients will pick a man's voice first.

What do you look for in the talent besides their voice quality?
I like a person to be flexible, show me a range of voices within their quality. Someone easy to work with and on time!

Do you have a lot of "on site" casting?
In smaller markets we do. We even cast through the talent in non-union gigs, but with the bigger markets, we work more so with the CDs or tape

How do you categorize women in voice-overs? How do you think that the client categorizes women in general when casting?
Unfortunately, we really tend to categorize women in one of three ways. It just seems to be that is what women constantly fall back on. Either they are sweet announcers, little girls or sexy. I really think that you opened up a whole new world for women. All the sudden women could be more accessible, likable and still have character. Your voice quality definitely brought a quirkiness to female voice-overs that had not been around before. You changed the way that I thought of women being cast. I think you did that for a lot of advertising agencies and clients.

Well, thank you.
When you are good at what you do, copywriters tend to re-hire the same people. It's easier to work with the same person. Most of the time, the client doesn't know Sally Smith from Joe Jones so they really don't care who we pick as long as the voice fits the spot we are doing.

Any final quote or thought?
Don't be late!

> *Every time I finish a job with an ad agency, I send then a new demo tape. They can never have too many. I cold-called one day in San Francisco when I was there for a job. I must have hit 25 ad agencies. Not one person saw me. But I made connections. I asked who the creative and copywriter were and left a tape. Sooner or later it may lead to a job.*

WHAT THE AD AGENCY DOES

Once an ad agency has been hired to do the job, their work begins. They work with the client to create the spot or campaign. The client may or may not have an idea of what the campaign should be. If not, it is up to the agency to come up with the campaign.

Depending on size and clout, an advertising agency works like all other companies. The more money and contacts and talent, the bigger the accounts. A small company with a very creative and smart ad team may compete and win a large account, simply because they have the best idea.

Once the ad team at the chosen agency has been given the project, they start to create ideas based on information they've been given from the client on how they want their product to sell. The client will tell the ad agency who they want their market to be, what age range, who they are trying to sell to. In fact, many clients will pick their ad agency based on what they've seen the ad agency do before and if they think that ad a agency can get their product marketed productively. The creative team (the idea side of an agency) will come up with a campaign or slogan and work from there. They work with the client to make sure that the client is happy. Depending on if it is television or radio they make the story boards, edit, copy and sometimes use someone in the ad agency's voice just to show to the client.

Once the copy is approved by the client, then they begin the casting session. The ad agency will call agents and casting directors in town to set up auditions. The agency sends them the copy and that is where you come in to do your work.

Writer

Once the creative team and the writer(s) come up with an idea, it is up to the writers to put the actual words on paper. Most likely, the writer will direct your voice-over session. However, you may be directed by the creative director, who will be at the session making sure you are hitting the words they want emphasized, or getting the rhythm right. Most of the time, the whole group will have been working closely on the campaign, and all will have a feel for what the client wants.

Producer
The producer is also the creative director. They oversee everything.

Director
The director is the creative director and may also be the writer. They will be at the session.

Account Supervisor
The account supervisor is that one who oversees the account and is the liaison between the ad agency and the client. They keep everything in line, make sure that budget is on target and the work is getting done efficiently. The account supervisor may be working for the ad agency or for the client. They may be at the session as well to make sure that all is running smoothly.

Talent
You, as the talent, may be hired for a job and then the job may get canceled. It could have to do with anything from changing the strategy, budget no longer available, client has creative differences than that of the agency, another agency got them away with a better idea, or they went with a different voice. You may be hired, and even then, you do not have the guarantee that the spot will run even if they tell you it is a national network. That is the business. You still do the work and will get paid for the session. If it airs, you will get the residuals.

Client
Clients stay with an agency until they feel they want a fresh look. The agency will try to keep them if they feel they have different ideas, but the client may move on. This usually means that they will find new voice-over talent, as well. They may be trying for a different age group or market. When the new auditions come around, you still may be brought in to read, but you may not book the job.

If you are hired for a non-union job, the ad agency may be just a guy in jeans who wrote copy and was hired by Sam's Key Shop for one radio spot. Most likely, Sam didn't have the money to pay the ad agency and he hired a guy locally who has a studio to produce the spot. This is where non-union work comes in. This is a good way to get jobs in the beginning. Sam may have even written the spot himself. It might run for the thirteen weeks while Sam is promoting a "Buy 2 get 1 key free" special. This is very common in smaller markets where the clients don't have big budgets and may not hire ad agencies.

☞ *Read the ad magazines.* Ad Weekly, Ad Age, Ad News. *These are great, informative magazines that will keep you posted on who has just won which job, give you a good idea of the budget, and what is hot right now. It also profiles different creative executives and accounts that they are working on. Write their names down, and send them a tape. You never know!*

An Interview with . . .
ERIC SEASTRAND, Voice-over Agent for International Creative Management (ICM) in Los Angeles; Formerly a Manager in Chicago.

We talked a lot about the Midwest. I wanted to know, currently, what is happening in the smaller markets outside of New York and Los Angeles.

What is the main difference between working in Chicago and working in Los Angeles??
In Chicago it's much more one on one. There are fewer people making more money. The talent pool in Los Angeles is much larger.

What do you look for in talent?
Professionalism. In Los Angeles it seems to be more professional. Chicago talent dabbles more in it as a hobby. It's also harder to make a full time living at it there.

What would you suggest to someone trying to break in to voice-overs in the Midwest?
Determination. You have to want to do it. You have to want to make it a career and it has to be a priority! New talent can make it anywhere—a diamond in the rough. It is getting harder, though, as the market expands. The business is much more competitive.

How important is a tape in the Midwest?
It's important. I tell anyone, though, if you are going to take the time to put together a tape, make sure you do it right.

Is there a lot of non-union work in Chicago?
There is more non-union work in Chicago than Los Angeles and New York.

So that would be a good place for new talent to try their luck?
It's a great market. Non-union is a good way to get started. Smaller markets have a lot more room for non-union work.

How do you feel about voice-over classes?
It depends on what stage you are at in your career. It's always good to take classes from a casting director. It's a great way to get to know them and for them to get to know you.

Any animation work in Chicago?
Not animation, but besides the voice-over, there are industrials and promos (smaller elements), as well as commercials (on camera and voice-over).

CHAPTER 14

• • •
MARKETING YOURSELF
• • •

It's great to think about how to market yourself. What particular voice do you think you do very well? Which area of the voice-over field most excites you? If you had your dream, would you be on two animated series, have a regular promo gig for a television station or be a DJ?

These are the really important questions that you need to ask yourself? Pick an area you think you would be good at. Then pursue and put your focus on what you think you are best. Find appropriate classes. Don't spread yourself too thin.

Whichever area you choose to pursue on your road to voice-over stardom, you have to always take the appropriate steps. Practice, classes, demo tape, agent, work, marketing, incorporation, auditions, staying afloat and knowing what is current.

MARKETING STEPS
1. Get a demo tape, and make sure you have lots of copies to send out and hand out.
2. Make a "J-Card." (See "Demo Tapes," Chapter 7)
3. Take classes
4. Keep up on your business relationships.
5. Keep track of new contacts and send over a tape and note.
6. Keep accurate records of every audition, every job, agency.
7. Be original. Be different.

The whole point of marketing yourself is to SELL YOURSELF! I sold myself by being assertive and taking classes. I made phone calls, I got into as many auditions as I could, read as much copy as I could, copied every commercial on TV and radio and spoke them aloud as well as to this day when I see an adver- tisement in a magazine, I read the copy aloud. I love to hear how it would sound if it were an audition. It also teaches me to be better at what I do, every time that I do it. Even though I had an agent, I still hand delivered demo tapes to every casting director in town. I re-submitted a tape and learned the casting directors names. I wanted them to put a face to the voice. This way, when they think of who to bring in, they are more famil- iar with you. Once you get the agent, you still have to do the work. Make sure that all the casting houses know who you are. That is going to take a little marketing on your part. Since they get so many tapes, you will need to be a little unique in figur- ing out how to get their attention so that they will listen. For a long time, my J-Card said, "AN APPLE A DAY", with an apple surrounding my name. Hey, it stood out.

A DAY IN THE LIFE OF A VOICE-OVER CAREER

8:30 a.m. Get a call from my agent that my 11:00 a.m. job for "Mobil On The Run" has been moved up to 10:30. Call my commercial agent and move my audition for "Clorox" up to 12:00.

Have coffee, shower and leave.

9:00 a.m. First stop is ICM, my voice-over agency.

Sit and wait for copy. Someone hands me copy to look over. While I wait to go in and read, I look at the fol- lowing scripts:

Blue Cross/Blue Shield of Omaha-Radio copy. The di- rection says warm, authoritative, real.

Coco's - TV National. Direction says "sultry, edge, con- versational."

Sierra At Tahoe - Radio. "Fun, over the top, mid 20's."

Subway - TV National campaign - "Real, Off The Cuff, Intimate, Fun!"

Twenty-five minutes later I'm off to the Valley. (They rush me out of there because they know I have a ses- sion to get to.)

9:45 a.m.	Arrive at the Voicecaster office. I walk in and look for the Arizona Lottery copy I am supposed to read for. One television spot, one radio spot. I wait for a partner and an announcer and look at the copy. Direction says "conversational, tongue in cheek, not over the top. Female Helen Hunt, Male Paul Reiser." (This happens a lot. It's more the attitude that they base it on, not the voice. They want the relationship between the two people)
10:20 a.m.	I'm out of there. I jam over to my voice-over session, which is at least fifteen minutes away.
10:35 a.m.	I walk in five minutes late, check in and go into the recording booth. The sound engineer greets me and hands me the copy. I'm safe because the client hasn't even called in yet. It's a phone patch. I look at the copy, fill out my contract and AFTRA report for the radio spot and go into the booth. I'm doing three TV spots and one radio spot. We hook up with Arizona, where the ad agency is calling from and I get on with the producer. We do the session in twenty minutes.
11:15 a.m.	I'm off to my on-camera audition late. I get paged as I'm walking out the door. It's my voice-over agent. They have an audition for me at 1:30 across town in Santa Monica for Mattel. I hang up the phone and get in the car. (By the way, I got rid of my car phone two years ago. I was ringing up a bill of $600 a month. Obviously I spend all my time in the car. It was the only chance I got to return phone calls.)
11:45 a.m.	I'm now a half-hour late to my 11:15 appointment. I grab my headshot and go to the audition. It's for Subway, interestingly enough. That same morning I did the voice audition and now I'm doing the on-camera. Just think, If I book both, I'll earn double residuals!!!
12:50 p.m.	Long wait! Cruise through a drive thru burger joint and get on the freeway. I don't make it to my 1:30 until almost 2:00. I stop along the way to call my agent. "No problem," they say
2:00 p.m.	I read for Mattel and head back over the hill to the gym for a long workout which I feel too tired to do, and then go back home. On the way, I get beeped. Mattel wants me to come in the next day.

I book a time and hang up the phone. I get emergency beeped not five minutes later and am told to go to CBS to read for some promos. I head back across town.

5:15 p.m.   I wait in the lobby for about 30 minutes and go in. I demo for a new CBS show and go home. By now, I'm exhausted and I still have a 30 to 45 minute ride home depending on the traffic. (I should have forgone the stick shift.)

6:40 p.m.   Finally home to my waiting dog and another 127 miles on the odometer for one day!

By the time I wake up the next morning, it's a new day and I do it all over again!

Welcome to auditions!

It's a funny thing. You wait and wait and wait until you get to the place where you're finally auditioning. Then once you're in, you spend all day, every day, in your car running from one audition to the next. If you're lucky, it's a heck of a way to pay the bills. Not such a bad way to spend the day either. That is if you don't mind traffic! (In L. A. anyway!)

An Interview with . . .
CARROLL DAY KIMBLE, Carroll Casting, Los Angeles

How you go about the casting process?
First, the client calls me, then they fax over the script. I spend a lot of time imagining a voice for the spot. I listen to tapes. I remember voices of people who I've called in. My clients rely on me to bring in the ten or so best voices for the job. I usually don't put a lot of voices on the tapes—just ones I think could book it. Then I call the agencies and the talent comes in. If a casting director calls you in, you have a much better chance of booking the job.

How do you find the talent to bring in?
Usually through the talent agencies. I also have developed relationships with talent and will continue to bring them in if I feel they have read well.

Will you listen to a tape that someone has dropped off?
Sure. I prefer to go through an agent though only because if they book the job, I know exactly where to find them. Depending on the spot, sometimes I have to cast very quickly.

If you hear a tape you like, would you recommend the person to an agent?
Sure. If I hear something really unique, I may call Jeff Danis, (voice-over agent at ICM) and say, "Hey, you've got to hear this guy!" It's really helpful to be in the unions, though.

Do you have a stable of talent that you call in?
Yes. Every casting director has some talent they can rely on to deliver 100 percent every time.

How does one get in the stable?
Relationships develop over time. I like someone with range, someone who takes direction really well. Someone who brings life to the script! An actor who is passionate about what they do, how they read, will blow me away!

What do you like from an actor once they come in and read?
It's a casting director's dream to know that a talent can walk in and nail it on the first or second take.

Do you have any influence once the tape goes out? Influence as to whom they hire for the job?
Sometimes the client will call for my recommendation. Other times I might call them and say, "Hey, Terri Apple nailed that read." They may listen or not. Usually it's up to several writers and producers. Other times they will call me just to book the spot. I'll read it and begin my casting process and think of who to call in or book for the spot.

What kinds of things do you cast?
About ninety percent of my work is commercials and the rest is CD-ROMs and documentaries.

Does a client hire more than one casting house at a time?
Rarely. Usually that only happens if the first casting house couldn't find anyone suitable. Sometimes the casting specs will change as well.

Do you teach?
Actually I do, but I don't advertise. I teach privately to actors who want to sharpen a certain skill, enhance their reads. Sometimes I'll get an actor who just wants advice. Maybe they haven't been booking as much and want to know if anything is wrong. We work on the problem areas. A great announcer really needs some help on conversational reads. We'll work on the weaker areas.

What would you say to an actor who goes from being busy to slow and back again?
The business changes. Sometimes there are specific casting specs. They want a really raspy smoker's voice in a male or a smooth rasp-less voice in a woman. It depends on the client, the job, the season. Everything changes. Women with texture were in. Then they're not. Then it's back again. Just depends on what sells at the time to the client.

So, what's the philosophy for actors to follow?
Just keep working and practicing. The ultimate goal is to get out to the casting houses and read! I have a lot of people who ultimately book something because they came into my casting house. They may have not booked the initial job that they read for. Remember that the client works on more than one project at a time. They may go over an old tape for another job and think you are perfect for what they are currently are working on. You never know. It's all connected.

Any parting words of wisdom?
Try to get into the casting houses. It's very important to get out to all the houses to read.

CHAPTER 15

•••
STEREOTYPING:
VOICES THAT BOOK AND TRENDS
•••

I get asked all the time how the HomeBase voice came about: it is a very deadpan, flat read. When I went to the audition, the description was "flat, throw away, irony." My interpretation of the read is how I got the job. My read came out of creating a character and trying to give the advertising agency what they wanted. I didn't try to be anyone else. I just did ME in that character. I didn't over analyze or over-read it. I just came up with something that felt comfortable and different. And it worked. That led to me being stereotyped and I was the "voice." Clients would ask for a Terri Apple voice, or in the direction it would say a Terri Apple read.

What Is Stereotyping?

Stereotyping is . . . copying or using as an example, a particular voice or style of voice. When a voice becomes popular, advertisers ask for that voice or someone very similar. That is stereotyping. They may say, "Get me a Tom Bodett (MOTEL 6, flat, low-key) or "Get me a Jim Cummings" (deep delivery, strong). Although, Jim does several different characters and reads, he is known most for his strong, deep voice.

Stereotyping is . . . tricky. I got stereotyped after doing the HomeBase campaign. Before that job, I did a lot of high energy and business reads. After booking HomeBase, they started wanting me to do that quirky, raspy, dry, throw away read. I didn't realize I had created a new character for myself, nor did I know it was going to be so popular.

Stereotyping is . . . categorizing voices. It can be beneficial when you're hot: advertisers will want you for everything. When you're not, or when you're overexposed, you won't get hired—a least not with that voice. That's when you will need go another route, try different voices. Or, advertisers may want a voice similar to you in tone and character, just not you. Maybe they like the general character that you started, they just want someone to do it with less rasp or a higher pitch. Maybe they like the tone of your reads, but want a new person, a new sound. Even if they want someone like you, they may simply not want you.

☞ *The only solution I have to being stuck in a stereotype is to: Keep creating new ways to read! As long as you stay individual and not copy anyone, you will always work. Even if someone is stealing your sound, they cannot steal your voice. Someone may be able to ride the wave of your success for awhile, but when your style read is no longer "in," the person copying you is in trouble. Now what are they going to do, copy someone else? The point is to try to do what you do that makes you unique.*

Voices That Book

Ad agencies are always looking for voices that can enunciate, not slur the words and speak clearly. They look for a distinct sound, something different from the norm of everyday voices they hear. From time to time, you will be called in to read the "Regular Joe. " This is a style of read. Your voice was chosen because of the wonderful quality that you and your bring to the commercial. This doesn't necessarily mean that only weird or distinctive voices, book jobs. This means that any type of interesting quality that your voice may have, helps.

There are several types of voices that book jobs. That's what makes the business of voice-overs so exciting. Women with deeper, throaty voices stand out a lot and therefore work a lot. Quirky, higher pitched women stand out. Deep voiced, booming men, dominate the narration and promo market. But these are all generalizations. Certainly, everyone of these ideals, can be broken. Women do work in narration and promos and plenty of men have a deep throaty texture to their voice as well as higher pitched men. It does seem that deeper, lower voices, no matter the sex, work a lot. The ad agency seems to feel that the deeper voice is strong, assuring and can sell their product.

AM I DOING THE RIGHT KIND OF READ?

Unless you book that job, you'll never really know. There isn't a right and wrong for reading. There is only different. Every person who auditions for that particular spot, is given the same direction when they walk into the room. Every person auditioning may have a similar quality to their voice. The only difference is how you read it.

BECOMING THE TYPE OF VOICE THAT AD AGENCIES WANT

You can't spend your life trying to be what "everyone" else wants. However, what you can try to do is be the best at what you do. Often, ad agencies do not know what they are looking for until they hear it. When you see a mixed group of people all auditioning for the same voice, you get the distinct feeling that the ad agency doesn't know exactly what it wants yet.

WAYS TO BE MORE COMPETITIVE

Be professional. Make every audition the best that it can be by being ready. Take the audition process seriously. The audition is the only test that the ad agency and client have to hear your voice. Make sure that you treat the audition like a pre-job!

Take classes. Take every class that centers around the area you are interested in. Don't let your inexperience with microphones and copy reading keep you from booking jobs. Practice! Take classes! Work with other professionals!

Current tape. Make sure that your tape(s) in whichever area you are pursuing, is up to date. Don't send out tapes that are five years old with old copy.

Be available! Don't get an attitude with your agent like you have better things to do than audition and run all over town. Make sure that your agent knows you put voice-overs first. It has to be your priority, even if money is low. Take a night job, if you have to, so that you will have days free to audition. Missing auditions when your agent calls, gives them the impression that you are not taking it seriously. They will give the next audition to someone who is willing to compete.

Stay focused. Don't worry about taking over the entire voice-over business, it's not going to happen. There is a fortune to be made, but you're better off being a specialist. You're not going to be the *top* commercial voice-over artist, the *top* promo person and the *top* animation voice. There's too much work, not enough time and, until they clone you, not enough voice. Sticking to one general area will keep you focused and let people know that you are competitive for that area of work. Being competitive doesn't have to be a negative thought. Competitive means that you are in the game!

Stereotyped Voices: The Good News and the Bad News

You can become stereotyped if you become known for only that one voice that you do. When that voice plays on the air and gets a lot of air time, people may begin to associate you with only that character and will only want to hire you to do that one type of voice.

Becoming a stereotyped or "known" voice is a double-edged sword. Who doesn't want to be known in this business and make lots of money? Do you want to be known doing the same character over and over?

It will make you money but may keep you from working a lot in the future when that voice is no longer in, or when the ad world decides that character isn't hot anymore. The voice may not be hot based on dropping sales for the product. Or, they may simply want a new sound. When a client may decides it's time to change the ad campaign, usually everything changes, including the voice.

At the same time, not becoming known for a type of read, can be detrimental as well. Maybe you don't do several different voices or reads. That's okay. Not every voice-over actor has a range and can pull out 35 voices on command. Many are in the business just to pursue narration. This is wonderful because they are focused on one area. If this is the case, being typecast can be a very good thing. You will be hired because you are the best at what you do.

Does Everyone Become Stereotyped?

Every agent likes to categorize the talent so they are easier to sell. They may represent five high-pitched women in their 40s, six raspy sounding women in their 20s, four men with a deep announcer sound, and two hyper, raspy-sounding late teen boys.

Stereotyping is something that happens from the ad world, not within your own agency. Although your agent(s), and the casting director(s) will fit you into a category, they won't stereotype you. You only end up stereotyped after your voice is out in the broadcast world and you are selling several different products as the same character.

What If I Become Stereotyped and Work Less?

You're going to have to take a little break and stop doing the same type of voice-over work that you did before. This may mean less income for awhile, but you want advertisers to stop seeing you as only that one voice. Have your agent submit you for other types of reads. Let them know that you want to show you can do something other than what you are known for. This is very important. Even if you have the spot(s) running that you are stereotyped for, as long as another commercial is running where you are different, at least it shows you have range and can do something other than what you are known for.

Agents often categorize their clients as it is easier to push them. You have to show your agent you can do several different types of reads and characters; show them you can broaden your range and broaden their idea of what you can do. Who knows, maybe you'll start a stereotype in a whole new area!

An Interview with . . .
MICHAEL FREEMAN, Writer and Producer of Promos, Friedland Jacobs Communications, Los Angeles, California

---

Michael, explain exactly what promos are used for.
A promo is to help you stay tuned to that show. Promos create an image for a show.

How did you get your start?
I did the news promos at E! Entertainment for a year and then I went to Fox News doing the morning and evening promos as a writer-producer as well. Then I did freelance which led me to daytime, where I am now.

What is the difference between news promos and daytime promos?
News is a lot more fast paced. you have to really come up with the promos quickly. I liked it, but daytime is a lot less stress. The turn-around time for a news spot can be as little as an hour. When you are in the number two market in the country (Los Angeles), the promotion for the 11:00 news is what really counts. People generally watch the 8-10 o'clock news. We have to come up with some great promos to entice viewers to tune in for 11:00.

How do you know what to say when you write?
You have to know how to sell the newscast or show. More often than not, it's the voice of the news that will determine whether or not that viewer will stay.

Which brings me to the "voice." Is there a certain quality you look for?
They take what is there and make it better! Part of making it better is casting the right voice. The right voice generally fits the mood of the spot. When I am writing, I try to already hear the voice, think about how it will sound and go from there.

How do you write the spot? Are there basic guidelines you follow?
Sometimes yes and sometimes no. Creating an image, that is what it's about. Some clients will give you specific guidelines and other clients say "We don't know what we want, you tell us." The voice is crucial. It's all in the tone and attitude that people relate to. The voice has to go with the product. Some of the best campaign's have gone with the antithesis of the product and that is what made it successful. I try to think along the lines of what the client wants to say and then write the spot with that particular attitude or voice quality in mind.

Are promo voices "bigger than life"?
I look for tone and quality. It's very important that the person can act with their voice. I want to be able to hear the smile in their voice. That's really important to me. If I can't hear the smile I will most likely try to find it in someone who can.

Are you the only one at Friedland Jacobs casting the voices?
It's usually a committee, myself and the client, but I also sell. Part of the job is to push certain clients, try to sell the script the best way we can. We call ourselves a full service advertising and marketing agency. We pursue clients and they come to us to promote their show or product.

What if a talent wanted to send you a demo tape?
That's fine. I'll listen to it. For me, anyone can fake a deep voice. If there is something different then I notice. I look for a quality that will make people stop and listen to the promo that they are hearing. I want people to stop and say "Hey, what's that coming out of my TV?" I don't like a sound that blends in.

What is the point of a promo?
The whole key to promos is to have people NOT flip the channels. You want them to look and listen to your spot.

How do you know they are listening?
We buy a certain number of spots (media buy), which guarantees a certain amount of airtime. If the show did well the week before, it may get more airtime. The more desirable the show, the tendency to run the promos. Basically a show with great numbers (Neilson ratings-how many people are watching the show) generates more revenue and the more people who watch means more money. It's up to the station to run which promos and how many, after the agreed upon media buy.

So, talent does NOT get residuals for network promos?
No. If they do six promos they get paid for six. Talent is paid per spot not per number of times aired.

What is the difference between network and syndication for commercials or promos?
Network is prime time shows. Networks. ABC, NBC, CBS, FOX. Syndication is a show that is sold to whatever market will buy the show.

Okay, let's talk for a minute about the actual session with the talent.
First and foremost, acting is the key. It's very important.

And what about timings? How important are they?
Once you get the voice, tone, attitude and quality, then the timings are really important. You have to know how to fit the words in the time before the next sound bite comes in. You need to know how to match the attitude with the attitude of the promo, which is where the acting comes in.

What's a sound byte?
The sound byte or SOT (Sound on Tape) is the actual scene that is going. Other actors voices will be on the tape. Your voice will go around around and between their words. You do the voice-over around the soundbyte. An example:

Promo Talent: "Last week on *Caroline In The City,* Caroline gets evicted",

(SOT) Caroline: "I don't know what I'm going to do Richard"

How do you feel about talent being on time? Helping with direction?
I don't mind if they are late and they call. Things come up.

Should they help with direction?
I don't mind direction if I know the person and I trust what they say. We need to be able to do our jobs though. Basically, though, talent should go in as talent. They are paid to do a job. We listen to ideas, but we pay talent to say what we want them to say, do what we want them to do. In the daytime promos I am doing now, acting is definitely more important. In news promos, I noticed that less acting ability and a good voice is fine for that. I can't stress enough though how the acting is so important. It's tough to get someone who can act with their voice to the visuals.

Can you tell me the process of your job? From beginning to job?
I get an account, write the spot, submit to my boss, he makes changes, gives it back to me, I make the changes, submit it back to boss, he okays it, sends it off to client. They make changes. Send it back to me, then back to the boss. Then we hire the talent, do the session, send it back to the client for final approval and then . . . It goes on TV!

COMMON TERMS USED IN THE PROMO WORLD

SOT - Sound on Tape or Soundbyte

GFX - Graphics

SFX - Sound Effects

TAGOUT - The wrap up for the promos. Ex:

> *"Judge Judy. She's ready to rule"*

> *"Real cases, real people, real judge"! (The end line they always use for that particular show. The line they are known for)*

TUNE IN TIME - When people are supposed to tune in

TIMINGS - Reading to picture and fitting in the timing of the Voice-over read to the SOT.

TO THE PICTURE - Term used to read the copy to the television spot that is airing.

"I NEED YOU TO OPEN IT UP" - Stretch more time to talk

TIGHTEN IT UP - Quicker read, need to get it in faster amount of time.

SPLIT THE DIFFERENCE - An acting direction to try for the middle of the last two reads that you did. Somewhere in between.

CANS - Headphones

GIVE ME A LEVEL - Read some of the copy at the tone and level we will be recording to so I can adjust the headphones and microphone. A technical term.

WE'RE SPEEDING - We're rolling tape. We're getting ready to record.

GRAPHIC UPPER 3RD - Top 1/3 of the TV set. Where the station puts the name of the show. The way that the graphics is placed on the TV by the station.

GRAPHIC LOWER 3RD - Where the station will put times and the logo for the station. The lower 3rd is reserved for the station ID.

I SMELL AN EMMY - The classic opposite. There is no Emmy for promos. A response to a really cheesy read or spot!

CHAPTER 16

• • •

THE UNIONS

• • •

I got fined for not sending in my AFTRA report within 48 hours. I had to go in and meet with their Board of Directors and explain why I was too lazy to mail in my report. I got fined $20. They want to teach you to follow the rules. They won't fine you right away, I got a few warning letters for not filing in the past, this time they fined me and made me go in to meet them. It taught me that I need to send in my report immediately after a job so that they will always have a record of my work to protect me. If the job plays without me knowing it, they will have a record and can contact the ad agency so I can collect my residuals.

There are two unions that you need to be concerned with: American Federation Television and Radio Artists (AFTRA) and the Screen Actors Guild (SAG). They both cover voice-overs as well as on-camera work. Generally, SAG is the union for film work and AFTRA covers videotaped projects (day-time television and syndicates shows). Electronic media (audio books, CD ROMS) may be covered by either union, it depends upon the contract.

If you want to join AFTRA, call your local chapter (see Appendix) and go join. They will give you all the details that you need to know. Then if you still haven't work within SAG by a year, you can join SAG. That's one of the perks. The only two ways to get into SAG is by joining and being a current paid up member of AFTRA for a year, or by getting a job that is SAG. You don't have to work in AFTRA to be a member. It's up to you, but remember, try to stay non-union as long as you can to build your resume. If the "big guys" really want you for a union job, they will hire you and you can join then if you want!

AFTRA and SAG are there to protect your rights as a performer, whether on-camera or off camera. Eventually, you want to be in both unions so that your work is protected and you are paid appropriately. You don't want to do non-union work the rest of your life, unless you don't mind being low-paid. Non-union performers are usually paid lower rates than union performers. Plus, the employer doesn't have to pay benefits and residuals. This is why a company will hire a non-union performer. They know that you need the work, the experience, the tape and that you will work for less money. If they had the budget to hire a union person, they would.

Bottom line—the unions are to help you. They have a retirement fund, a credit card, health and retirement plans (if you earn enough each year), and any time you are confused and have a question regarding a job, joining, rates, other performers or anything else you can think of, they will be happy to answer it.

American Federation of Television and Radio Artists (AFTRA)

You can join AFTRA in any town at any time. (See Appendix for list of AFTRA chapter offices.) They will be happy to take your money. At this writing, dues are around $800. If you are in a major market such as Los Angeles, New York or Chicago, membership will cost a little more. It is less expensive to join in the other markets; you will need to join wherever you live and work. Once you begin working in another market, you will need to transfer your membership to that local chapter.

While AFTRA only requires that you sign up and pay your dues, SAG is a little harder to get into. Once you have been a member of AFTRA for a year or have worked on two SAG project s within thirty days of each other, you are eligible to join SAG. Once you are a member of either union, you cannot legally accept non-union work. If you do and you are caught, you can be fined and thrown out of the union.

Benefits of Joining AFTRA

If you are in, you can make sure that you are paid the union scale—the minimum salary for voice-over work. You will be doing higher quality work. And you will be protected by a union to make sure you are covered for your benefits. (Note: you need to reach a certain level of earnings before these benefits apply.)

When you're a member of AFTRA a year, you can join SAG. This makes it easier if you get hired for a SAG job—you will already be a member.

If a company wants to hire you for a union job and you're not union, they can hire you under the Taft-Hartley Law. This means that you can still do the job without having to join the union. If, however, you book another union job within 30 days, you will have to join the union. If you book a non-union job within those 30 days, you are fine. You don't have to join the union until you book 2 union jobs within 30 days of one another.

> *Taft-Hartley Act: With respect to actors, the Taft-Hartley Act states that a non-union actor can be hired by a union producer or production company. The actor then has thirty days to join the union.*

Unions and Harassment

If you are harassed at a job, call the union. They will make sure to do a report against the person who you had a problem with.

> *The only problem I have ever encountered, was when I was called in to do a demo for a commercial. I went to the session and the writer was still playing with several different options. He had me read about 15 different lines. After that, he asked me to come up with lines. Once in awhile in a session, you will ad lib or help come up with a better word if nothing seems to be working. The writer doesn't generally mind your saying a word that works better than one they picked. This was different because this was an entire line. He wanted my help in matching the picture to a line. That was his job and I called my agent. They were not paying me to write the spot, only to do the voice-over. When I called my agent, he was furious that they were using me in that way. I hung up with him and he called the writer, who promptly had me just read the original lines that he had written.*
>
> *The story has a happy ending because the commercial ran and made lots of money. Make a judgment call if the session does not seem to be going according to what you know.*

Unions and Paperwork

Once you are a member of the union, you need to fill out the proper form after each job that you do. You then need to send a copy of the AFTRA Form to the AFTRA office within 48 hours of doing the job. SAG does not require this. If you don't, AFTRA will fine you $20. This is to protect you from not getting paid and keeps that union up on what you are doing. They want to make sure that the job was union and that you are paid in a timely manner. You should be paid within one to two months from doing your job. If you aren't tell your agent, or call the union.

If there is no contract when you are done with your job, the studio should have appropriate forms. Fill them out. Send them in. Send a copy to the ad agency. Call your agent and let them know. Maybe the contract will be sent to them. To be safe, it doesn't hurt to fill out a contract anyway for your own records.

UNION TELEPHONE NUMBERS IN LOS ANGELES:

SAG Information	*(213) 954-1600*
SAG Health Union	*(818) 954-9400*
SAG Credit Union	*(213) 461-3041*
AFTRA Information	*(213) 634-8200*
AFTRA Health Union	*(213) 937-3631*
AFTRA Credit Union	*(213) 461-3041*

SAG and AFTRA Pay Scales

Note: These rates are current as of the last contract negotiation which occurred in 1997, which will stay in place until the year 2000. They renegotiate every three years. AFTRA and SAG negotiate together, as they are sister unions. Often, their rates are the same.

Each commercial runs on a thirteen week per spot/per cycle basis. The total lifespan of a commercial runs 21 months. This means your commercial can run in thirteen-week segments during the 21 month period. After that, your contract expires. The agency can no longer run the commercial without re-negotiating with you or agent.

You will be paid a scale fee for recording the commercial. If it is radio commercial, you will only get paid once every thirteen weeks. They may run the spot several hundred times within the thirteen weeks, and you will still only be paid once. If it is a television commercial, depending on the market (national, regional, local) you will be paid the thirteen week session fee and then residuals. The residual rate will vary with the market. National commercials are, obviously, the best paying spots.

AFTRA (Basic Minimum Rate of Pay)
$185.00 plus ten percent. This means that your agent's fee, in this case $18.50, is paid in addition to your rate. Overscale is considered to be payment in excess of $325.00.

SAG (Basic Minimum Rate of Pay)
$333.30 (ten percent comes out of the $333. 30.) The plus ten per cent is according to what the agent has negotiated. With SAG, this ten percent is not automatically added to your fee. If it is not negotiated, you will need to pay your agent his ten percent from your fee.

Below are listed different "exposures" of commercial usage; different ways in which advertisers (buyers) purchase media time. The unit weight (announcement of usage, type of usage) determines your pay scale for spot(s) and how much you will be paid.

Class A National Network
Use #1:	$333.30
Use #2:	$96.00
Uses #3-13:	$76.35 each
Uses #14 +:	$34.65 each

These fees are for each use. You will also be paid your "session" fee. So if you see your commercial has run 17 times, you will be paid almost $1,300. If your commercials is picked up for another 13 week cycle, you will be paid another session fee, and the rate will start at the top again. If they don't run the spot again, but don't want to cancel it, you will be paid a holding fee.

Non-Air Demo Rate for AFTRA or SAG
$166.65 plus ten percent, negotiable with agent. If, after you've done a demo and if it gets upgraded to broadcast, you will be paid the appropriate scale fee, including residuals, if applicable.

The ad agency will let you know if the spot goes from demo to broadcast. There is a broadcast division of the unions that keep track of how often your commercial has run and make sure that you get your residuals. Sometimes a radio spot that has been broadcast, can slip through and you won't know that it played. Radio is much harder to keep track of. Ask your friends and relatives to let you know if they hear your commercial. If you haven't been paid for it, call AFTRA and they will track it down for you.

Tags
$96 for each of the first 12 tags, then $76.60 each tag thereafter.

Wildspot
This is a form of residual that covers thirteen weeks of unlimited use in the market purchased. The commercial may have only run in two or three markets or as many as they want. You are paid a wildspot use rate. It is for unlimited use.

National, 4 weeks:	$603.35
National, 13 weeks	$1192.55
Regional, 13 weeks	$719.65
Non-Air, Demo:	$127.60

Other Rates

Narration (per hour):	$311.00; thereafter, per half hour. increment $91.00
Narrator spokesperson:	$691.00 first day; thereafter $380.00
Animation scale:	$504.00 per every three voices. Thereafter, an additional fee
Dubbing, looping:	$522.00 for five lines or more TV, MOW, film, residuals based on airing.
Promos	$215.00 per promo, per thirteen week cycle.

Markets

Local:	The spot(s) will run only in the one city that your contract specifies.
Regional:	The spot(s) will run in a number of cities, from two to twenty depending on the market. You will be paid accordingly.
National:	This will run all over though not necessarily on Network television
Cable:	Running on Cable channel. Paid cable or "wildspot" use
National Class A Network:	Runs on National television all over. Network Highest paid usage.
Wildspot:	Can run unlimited number of times in any city. Pays the wildspot usage fee

Usage

What you are paid for the commercial that is running. The usage is the amount of times and where it's played.

"Per Spot Per Cycle"

You must write this on every contract that you do next to the thirteen week rate (See example end of chapter) and next to your name. You want to make sure that you are paid every 13 weeks. They can run a commercial for a year, and you will still be paid every 13 weeks.

Holding Fee

This is a fee paid to you by an agency to hold you, but not run your commercial. You will be paid an additional holding fee every thirteen weeks until the commercial runs again, or is dropped.

Residuals

Residuals are where the bucks are! Residuals are standard with national, cable, regional and local TV ads. The difference lies in what the commercial ran. Residuals are automatic and you will receive them every week or so. You are paid residuals every time your commercial plays. If the commercial runs longer than 13 weeks, you are re-paid along with more residuals.

Conflicts

In radio, there are none. You can have a BMW, Cadillac and Toyota running at the same time. The only problem is that the client may not want you doing all three and may not hire you. But it isn't illegal. You can do conflicting things, no problem.

Television is different. Any two products that are competition, are a conflict. You cannot do two cereal companies: No Quaker Oats and Kellogg's. You cannot do Nike and Reebok. You can do a car, a cereal, a feminine product commercial, a beer and a soda. Those are all different. If you have a radio spot that's Reebok and you get a national Nike, that is okay. There is no conflict between radio and TV. Just TV and TV.

It's not your fault if you are hired to do two shoe commercials, the problem is, you can't do them per union rules. As well, ad agencies don't want you selling two products that are in competition. You may get called to audition for two shoe commercials, but if you have an agent, they probably won't send you in to read for it, knowing you have another shoe commercial on TV running. Now, if the commercial has run its 21 month cycle, you are free to audition for the other commercial that would have normally been in conflict.

An ad agency has to pay you a holding fee (In a sense, hold you for however long they may want to run the commercial, even if they don't run it for 3 months). In that time, if you book another commercial that would be a conflict, you will need to turn it down if you have been paid the holding fee from the other company. This is their security that you won't go do another job for a competing company.

It may seem unfair to struggling actors who are in the union and don't work a lot. They may think, "It's so hard, just to get one job, but then I get another and I can't even do it." Sorry, I, as the actor, would love to do as many jobs as I possibly can, but the union has its own rules and we've got to follow them.

You may be fined and thrown out of the union if you are caught doing two same like television spots. Now if the television spot is not national and you have a local Toyota in San Francisco and they also want you for a Jeep Cherokee in the East, that is fine. You just can't have two television Car spots running in the same market at the same time. You would need to wait until they release you (let go of the commercial) before you are free to pursue other car ads.

Non-Union

Non-union work is big in smaller markets and smaller cities. There is still plenty of non-union work in bigger cities too. Many industrials and low budget radio spots use non-union actors. If the client and agency or individual doesn't go union, the work can still be good. It's pocket money for you and it's tape. Take all the non-union work that you can get until you are forced into the union. There is a lot more work out there for beginners in non-union.

> *I built up a lot of non-union work so that by the time I became union, I knew exactly what I was doing. I scanned local papers looking for industrial companies hiring. I called the local production facilities and sent out tapes. I dropped off demo tapes to ad agencies and radio stations. I dropped off demo tapes to the theater and Radio, TV, Film departments at the local junior collage and collage. I began to get calls and went to audition, which eventually led to jobs.*

When you are doing a non-union job, you can name your fee. If a company isn't signatory with a union and you are not in a union, you can take the job and negotiate your fee. Remember what scale for union is, name your fee and see if they go for it. A lot of people do non-union work for anywhere from $50 to $200 depending up on the job. If they want you all day for a whole project, ask for more. Industrial non-union projects still pay pretty well. You could probably get around $200 to $400 for a day's work. Not bad!

• • •

CHAPTER 17

THE SOUND ENGINEER AND THE SOUND STUDIO

• • •

> *I was doing a session with a very cranky sound engineer. The session was long, and he was not a happy camper. Well, there were a couple of us in the booth and a few said some not so nice things, which the sound engineer heard. Always take off your headphones when saying "not so nice" things about people. The headphones pick up everything.*

THE SOUND ENGINEER

A good working relationship between you and the sound engineer is of high priority. They are the ones working with you in the session, whether the client is there in the room or not. The sound engineer works for the studio. When you book your job and show up, the sound engineer has been "assigned" to you and your session. There may be several sound engineers at each place you work. You may work with the same sound engineer over and over again, throughout the years. The sound engineers studio is basically his office. You are entering their world. They have the levels and keyboard set up exactly how they need it. They know everything from the phone patch to the editing process.

Their computer keyboard allows them to control all the technical aspects of the session: from making sure that your headphones work correctly, to setting up all the equipment, to keep track of all the reads. Sometimes they will play director and help all along with certain reads. They are a very valuable and important part of the process in the session and editing. They are responsible for the music, sound effects, timing, editing and looping of a spot. Either the ad agency has brought in a music track that they want to use or the sound engineer will take a track from their massive collection. They also may be doing the sound effects for the read.

The sound engineer is the one doing all the technical aspects of the session. They are in charge of hooking up the phone patch, getting you and the client/ad agency comfortable while making sure that you sound good and the session goes smoothly. If you haven't gotten the picture, the sound engineer is very important to the voice-over actor. Treat them with respect.

THE SOUND STUDIO

The booth is the room in which you do your voice-over. There will be microphones, a stand, and perhaps a chair. The sound engineer will tell you which stand and mike you are hooked up to for your work. The copy will either be on the microphone stand or will be in the other room and you will bring it in with you.

Here's what you will find in the booth:

Microphone: This will be a standing mike which the sound engineer will adjust it. Don't touch it, it's against policy. They will move it to fit you. Let them know if you need it to be higher, lower, etc. If you are working with a group, there will be individual mikes set up with their own stands. Once the mikes are set, the engineer will then go into the other room and get a level on your voice.

Their computer keyboard allows them to control all the technical aspects of the session: from making sure that your headphones work correctly, to setting up all the equipment, to keep track of all the reads. Sometimes they will play director and help all along with certain reads. They are a very valuable and important part of the process in the session and editing. They are responsible for the music, sound effects, timing, editing and looping of a spot. Either the ad agency has brought in a music track that they want to use or the sound engineer will take a track from their massive collection. They also may be doing the sound effects for the read.

Headphones: These will be supplied for you along with a level adjuster. (The adjuster may just be with the sound engineer and you will then ask them to adjust it) otherwise you have your own control to sound louder, softer or whatever you want.

Filters: These will either be cone shaped or screen shape square or round. According to the type of read, these will be on the mike for your voice. They will be for slurring, popping of P's or clarity. The sound engineer puts these on ahead of time or after you begin the read if they feel it's appropriate

Time Clock: This may or may not be in the room. If it is, it will be set up in the window between you and the sound engineer so that you can see the timing of the read as you go along. Otherwise, after each take, you will be told the time as you go. (You may choose to bring a stopwatch, but in a session, don't follow it, just work with the director. The stopwatch may confuse you)

The Stand: This is just a music stand adjustable from the floor up and tilted back. You can adjust the stand the way that you want it and the sound engineer will adjust the mike around that.

An Interview with . . .
BOB STEWART, Sound Engineer

Stewart Sound Factory is located in Irvine, California. His sound engineering business consists of voice-overs, CD-ROMs, music videos and industrial films. He does quite a bit of work in Orange County and deals directly with producers/directors in Los Angeles and Orange County. His job is to technically advise the session as well as cut, paste and complete the spot. A normal day is anywhere from two to three jobs. Stewart Sound prefers to book out half-days, but will work hourly with client and talent.

If the client doesn't have a large music/sound effects budget, then Bob pulls from his CD library. Almost every imaginable sound can be found stored on CD. There are many names for the CDs such as; *Pro-Tools* (mixing and recording), *Studio Vision Pro-Integrated* (Audio Recording), *Cubase* (Music recording and editing software, *Soundedit 16, Logic Audio, Native Power Pack, Vision* (Studio reference guide*), Sound Ideas* (Sound FX library), *Hanna Barbera* (Sound FX library) *Fun! With Sound Effects.* And these are just a few. Imagine what you can pick from to complete your spot!

Everything is computerized now. When I started in voice-overs, spots were cut together by hand, everything was on a reel, and there was no such thing as a phone patch. Today, almost all work is done digitally. I observed the making of an actual Chevrolet commercial while I did this interview. Bob and his crew cut it to picture and sound that was set up on the computer. They put the entire commercial together, ready for air, in less than an hour!

I asked Bob a few questions about his business, while he was working on the Chevy spot.

What was your last big job?
I just did 74 Chevy spots in one day. Sent them off on DSS.

DSS?
Digital Sound System. It's very popular now. Gives very clear sound.

Are you more of a technical engineer or do you do any directing with the producer?
It depends on the client. Mostly I try to just do the technical aspect. The levels, the microphone, the sound edit board, showing the scratch track, working on the music. If the producer wants my opinion, they may ask for my advice, then I'll offer my input. By the time we get through a session, we may pull different takes from several different reads. Like in this one, we pulled the first line from take #2, the next three lines from #14, the next one line from #37, and the tag from #7. That's very normal.

I noticed that you played it to the picture digitized on your computer. You edited it to the picture for sound and timing. Is this common?
That's very common now, if the producer brings along the spot. We can put it to music only, or to the picture or both.

Can you set it up for the talent to read to picture and sound, while they are in the booth?
Sure. Sometimes the producer wants it wild, though, to hear the read fresh.

What if the read is perfect, but just a fraction too long. Can you shorten it?
Through the computer, we can do something called "time compression." We can cut a spot, make it tighter, pull out the air. We used to do this physically by cutting the actual film or tape. Now we can basically, digitally, pull out the air. You won't even notice the time difference missing.

Can you do the same for stretching the read?
We can put air in, buy some time if we need to. Say a second or so.

What's a "slot mix?"
That's the music mix that the producer wants for the spot that has been pre-mixed by the sound engineer.

What happens if the session is completed, the talent has already left and the producer wants to change something?
We have a master copy of the spot, along with a copy that goes to the producer. As far as time is concerned, they call and book "pick-up" time. It's less expensive than the full hour, but they may need to have the talent come back in or phone patch for the pick up line.

I noticed that you showed the talent the scratch track before the producer got to the session. Is that common?
It depends on the spot. If the spot is there to show and I have the copy, I'll show it to the talent. It will help make the session go easier and gives the talent an idea of where to go with the copy. If I have music cut already, I will maybe put it all together for him/her. It depends on the time frame and the producer.

I see that you also do CD-ROMs?
Yes. We have a huge CD-ROM company in Orange County called Interplay with an in-house editing facility. Often they are so overbooked, they use outside studios. CD-ROMs are very big business.

How do you feel about receiving tapes from talent?
I'll listen to them. If a company is looking for a voice and hasn't cast the spot yet, I may recommend someone from our shelf. We always listen to new talent. We do a lot of industrial jobs which will occasionally use non-union talent. A CD-ROM company called us last week to ask about any female voice-over talent that we knew, so we hold on to all voice tapes that we receive.

Will you work with the talent at all, help them along in the session?
Timings are important. It depends on the level of talent. Of course, I will always be helpful if I can, trying to get them to do the spot in time, work on levels, getting the read that the producer wants. That's all part of the job! If we feel that a second to relax will get the talent back into the mode of the spot, it works well. Anything to help the session run smoothly for the talent and the agency!

CHAPTER 18

• • •
WHAT TO DO IN LOS ANGELES
• • •

I moved to Los Angeles in 1987 and wasn't sure what the voice-over market would be like. I found out who the agents were by calling the unions. I picked up a list of agents and began mailing out my demo tape with a note, "New in town. Enclosed is my demo tape."

Through the agencies, I found out who the casting directors were and sent out tapes. I called, I dropped off and I waited. I went on auditions and got an agent to send me out. Los Angeles may be a big town but the voice-over market is small. Make sure that you are ready and that you know what your doing. There are very few casting people and fewer agents. You don't want to show them an unpolished side. Be prepared and be business minded.

GET AN AGENT

When approaching agents, it is best to mail a demo tape along with a letter. A resume of your work can be included on an attached sheet of paper (see sample submission letter at end of this chapter). The letter should be short and professional. Call the agent first to find out the name of the appropriate agent. Either it will be an assistant or the voice-over agent.

Call the agent or assistant after a few days and make sure they received the tape. If you are in the area, drop off the tape in person instead of mailing it. You might get a chance to say hello in person, so the assistant or agent can put a face with the name. They might listen to the tape and get back to you. Call them within one week. If they listened to the tape and are passing, ask any advice. Do they know where you can take a class? A smaller agency? Any advice on changing the tape? If you get one answer from every person who you meet, this will help you learn as you go when you are entering a new city and know no one in the voice-over business.

Some agents re not be to listen to new tapes. If you call them and they tell you they aren't accepting any new submissions, thank them and call another agency. There is always the possibility that an agent loves your tape, but they already represent someone who sounds very similar to you—conflict of interest. Their loyalty will lie in trying to get the signed client work. Don't let this get you down. A lot of agencies represent talent who sounds similar or who will go out for competitive parts. Just keep plugging away.

If you feel rejected, take a class, take a break and start over. In the meantime, Los Angeles is a great training ground. There are many casting directors and classes. Also, there are so many student films, and other types of voice-over work. Read the local trade papers. This would include all the entertainment publications for that city or state, casting magazines, *Backstage West/East, Hollywood Reporter, Variety*, the local college paper and magazines like *Ad Week.* Voice-over jobs for industrials, commercials and films are always listed there.

Cover all the Casting Houses

While you are looking for an agent (and once you have one as well), send your tape out to all the casting houses. The routine is the same: Mail out your tape with your submission letter. Enclose a resume if you have one. Call in a few days to make sure the tape arrived. Reintroduce yourself and ask if you can come in and read for something. If not, ask them to please keep you in mind. Start relationships. Get to know people.

It's not a bad idea to spend an afternoon taking the casting directors a basket of cookies along with your tape. Use a reputable gift basket company, like Ms. Beasley's or Miss Grace's. Introduce yourself, re-introduce yourself, or just say hi, if they haven't brought you in to read in awhile!

Submit to Advertising Agencies, Production Companies and Promo Houses

OK, by now you've definitely got the picture on what to do. To submit your tape to advertising agencies, production companies and promo houses, follow the same guidelines as listed above with one exception: don't make the follow-up call, especially if it's just a general submission. The person receiving your tape will listen to it time permitting. You may or may not ever hear from them. Keep a running list of people you've met over the years and contacts you've made. Add this person to your list. Send them a card at holidays. Send a note once a year with a list of your new commercials you have running.

If someone at an ad agency specifically asks for a copy of your tape, submit it along with the note. Then it's OK to call and make sure they got it. They may not have anything for you at the time, but you never know.

When you've submitted your tapes, you will not get them back! They now belong to the person to whom you have sent your tape. This is why you keep a lot of demo tapes and why you have a lot made. Demo tapes cost about $1 per tape, less if you have more made.

SAMPLE RESUME

BETH JONES
Voice-over Agents Unlimited
SAG/AFTRA
310-555-1234

Animated Films/TV Series

Duckman	Special Guest
Rug Rats	Bobby
South Park	Butterfly Lady

Commercials

Pizza Hut	National TV
Tina's Nail Salon	Local Radio

If you have a list a page long, list the spots, commercials, animation and promo jobs you've done. A resume is not necessary in voice-overs. That is why you have your demo tape. If you do on-camera and voice-over, you may want to have a list that you have attached for voice-over jobs separate. When you meet with a voice-over agent, you can bring your resume along with your demo tape or tell the agent the jobs that you've done. If you've only done one or two jobs, don't worry about writing out a list. Tell the agent when you see them. Most likely, those spots will be on your demo tape.

Refer to the Appendix for a list of agents, casting directors, production houses, advertising agencies, etc. Use the list. Work the list. Make it work for you. And, if I haven't said it enough times already, get into a class, make a tape, and begin!

SAMPLE SUBMISSION LETTER

```
(Date)


Ms. Pam Smith
Voice-over Agents Unlimited
555 Wilshire Boulevard
Hollywood, CA 90000

Dear Pam,

Per my conversation with your assistant, Brad,
enclosed is my commercial demo tape. I am
currently seeking voice-over representation.
I recently moved from Ohio where I did several
regional and national voice-overs.

Thank you for your consideration and I look
forward to speaking with you soon.

Sincerely,



Beth Jones
310-555-1234
```

CHAPTER 19

•••
MEN VS. WOMEN
•••

> *On a daily basis I fight the men-women prejudice in the voice-over world. I happen to disagree that men get "all the work." I happen to get a lot of the "male voice-over" work. I make sure that my agent sends me out on men copy because my voice, which is lower and raspy, gets to compete more with men. I have booked a lot of jobs that were originally intended for men. I don't like to feel like I can't book the same amount of work, so I created a market where my voice (along with other women) could be up for the same kinds of jobs. I like knowing that I am fighting the men in what people consider to be the man's world of voice-overs.*

The man vs. woman voice-over debate exists. But so does the man vs. woman issue in every part of our economy and our world. Where it comes into play into voice-overs is the area that we want to address. Any given day that you will audition for copy, there will also be men auditioning—sometimes for the same copy, sometimes for different. There is a belief that men do most of the work. As I said above, I don't believe it and I will expose some common myths and fallacies about men and women in the voice-over world.

The narrator can be a female. Usually, narrators have lower pitched voices: a voice that sounds more commanding; a voice that people will easily listen to as the "information" person; a voice that says, "I know what I'm talking about, so please listen to me." Some higher-pitched women complain that they don't get called for announcer spots. However, these same women also book lots of funny, airhead spots, as well as a ton of animated work. This isn't a gender issue, it's a voice issue.

If you have an enlightened (no gender bias) agent, she will begin to let you read outside your normal reads. She will also give you "male" copy. If she is creative, she will understand that as long as you are reading and interpreting copy the way the ad agency wants, you have a real shot for the job. It never hurts to try.

Men still make more money on the whole, but that's true in all jobs, unfortunately. Several successful voice-over women make over a half a million dollars annually, but it's from doing several animated cartoon series, some animated films, and plenty of commercials, campaigns and promos.

A man can make a million a year from one network promo contract, alone. Men tend to book those promos more. Nighttime networks like to use men to bring mass audiences in. Men can make more money from work because they can make the money in one area. Although in animation, men and women do a lot of voices, there are still more animated shows for men's voices.

SOME COMMON FALLACIES

Men Work Much More than Women
Men work a lot, but so do women. So do kids. The market isn't one sided, except that there are certain areas where one sex works more.

Women Only Do 20 Percent of All the Voice-over Work
Although there are no published statistics, the reality seems to be more 60/40, with men dominating. The men still have the lead in being "the voices we listen to." Don't be too hasty to "blame society" for this situation. The advertising world goes a long way to perpetuate t his. And take a look at the world out there: men still have most of the so-called "important" jobs. We're not here to debate men vs. women in life; you just need to be aware of how it affects the voice-over world.

There is work out there. Women make up a large portion of the cosmetic and perfume market. We also make up a lot of the daytime products on television. Now it's true that men dominate at night. Just listen to your television. Women are moving up though. Men mostly are doing the promos for the networks and the evening ad's. Women are still working and doing products.

The best work wins! The best work that the ad agency, producer, director and writer choose, that is!

This doesn't mean that an advertiser doesn't have a specific voice or sexual orientation in mind, but they can also be swayed in the other direction if they are at least open to seeing either gender. Usually what will happen is that they will hear a voice that seems to go with the product they are selling. If the way in which you interpreted the copy and the quality of your voice go with what they are trying to say, you could easily get the spots or campaign over another gender. This goes both ways though. A man could get the job from a woman. But since there are more jobs for men out there, women want to try to get a fair shake.

I try to change the philosophy of men doing one type of voice-over and women doing another. I have been lucky enough to book (campaigns) that were previously "owned" by men: HomeBase (hardware), Blue Cross/California Care (health insurance), Mazda (car campaign), Carl's Jr. (burger campaign), Milk (campaign, they were initially looking for a man). This makes me feel good because we should and are starting to successfully cross over into all areas of voice-overs and be seen in a competitive light in the voice-over work.

Promos are the same thing. My agent told me women don't get a lot of work in this field, so I challenged that and made a promo demo tape. Next thing, I started booking CBS promos. They have used me quite a bit instead of a man. Not that I am trying to take work from anyone, but I'll take what they give me with pleasure! And I certainly like being up for a job regardless of sex. Sometimes a promo campaign will say "put a few women on there" and a woman will book the job. Interestingly enough, promo jobs that start out with women, end up using men. The networks just feel safer with a man's voice for a show. They feel that a man's voice is stronger and will pull in the numbers for a TV show they want a mass audience to watch. Women's voices to them, are still too "feminine or quirky." They see a woman's voice only as promoting a women's shows—daytime television. The powers that be feel safer putting women announcers during daytime programming because they feel that the woman will bring in other women.

Generally, networks believe that male voices bring in the mass audience. Numbers have always shown it, but they've never tried an evening of women doing promos either. They don't want to take the chance. Especially during a sports playoff. Then, you will only hear men's voices doing commercials or promos unless it's a sexy woman's voice that draws and brings in the man's attention. Did you ever notice that? It's very interesting, but pre-planned to lure the men in.

CREATING A MARKET FOR YOURSELF

Work with your natural range and tone. Don't stray too far (at least for commercial reads) from the natural sound of your voice. This doesn't mean that you shouldn't do characters, just don't forget to do what you do best. That very trait that sounds odd or interesting, may just get you the job and create a market for yourself.

TRAILERS

Men dominate the trailers. But that's because generally the films that sell the big bucks are male oriented and they want to push that. The female voice-overs you hear are usually for female type films which do not generally do as well at the box office unless it's a Sharon Stone film or Julia Roberts. Mostly the action packed films are done by men.

ANIMATION

A lot of females with a rasp to their voice do a lot of the little boys that you hear in animation. More and more though, they are going with kids. Real kids to do the real spots. This is new. They are starting to trust younger kids and hiring them, thus pushing the female/boy market to fewer jobs for women. Women have always done voice-over for the young boy roles. Men's voices are too deep and once their voice changes from boy to man, it becomes too obvious that they are trying to sound young.

LOOPING, DUBBING AND JINGLES

This depends on the character they are doing or singing. Nowadays, we hear so many different products and so many different types of voices. Who knows who is selling what! Advertisers will try anything. So don't be surprised if you are hired for something that you never thought you'd ever be hired for. Residuals, from any commercial, are Heavenly!

ADVICE FROM THE PROS

"I always used to carry around a list of the studios every time I got sent on an audition. I felt that somehow it made me more alert and better prepared."

—*Dave*

"I find that I like to read in the mornings, when my voice is deeper and throatier. By the afternoon, it seems to have smoothed out and I don't feel as competitive for the same kinds of roles."

—*Beth*

"When I'm preparing for an audition, and the copy is in front of me, I read through it two times first. Then I take a highlighter and highlight all the words I think should be said brighter or stronger. I also pre-plan which way the words are going to go at the end of each sentence, up or down. This helps me feel like I know what I'm saying when I go on in there to read."

—*Debbie*

"I get nervous when I see a lot of other people auditioning. I feel as though they'll like everyone except me. When I read, I sometimes try to disguise or change my voice, hoping they'll like that better than my natural sound. My agent inevitably calls me and tells me to go back to being me."

—*Kristen*

"I know that for every job, there's at least a room full of other men who could read that copy the same or better. I read the copy once, find a character out of my "pocket" of characters, and read the copy that way, no matter what the director asks for. At least I feel it makes me stand out and maybe I'll get the job because I was different."

—*David*

"I live in the Midwest, so I don't feel the sweat of competition so much. I'll basically be called directly to read for some part. When I do have to audition, I make sure and go over the copy several times, reading it different every time. I read the copy until I mentally tell myself that I am the only possible voice for that role, which makes me give a better reading. Thinking that another person couldn't possibly get that job, helps me make strong vocal choices."

—*Barbara*

"I just go in and be myself. I try not to think what another voice-over actor would do. The competition side of it freaks me out. If I thought about that all the time, I wouldn't be able to read the copy. A lot of these people are my friends, so of course, I want everyone to get the job. I just try to do what I do and wing it."

—Steve

"I do a lot of promo work, but I think it's because they hear a booming voice come through. I guess they like my delivery and I always pretty much do the same delivery. I don't put much emphasis on any words, I just read the copy with my voice. Other voice-over actors may put too much emphasis on words, make too much out of the promo, because they think that they need to sound loud or pushy. I think women are used more for intimate promos and daytime talk shows, where there is a more female audience. The networks and production companies like to use women more for day and men more for night."

—John

What did we learn here? Men work more? Women dominate with feminine products? The only judgment and competition you should feel, is with yourself. You are the only one that you have to worry about. There is nothing you can do about everyone else on an audition, how to "beat" them, do "better," or "win." These words don't even fit with a good audition. And you should never feel threatened by the gender issue. You are the gender you are and the work is out there, regardless. Don't worry about not booking that big promo campaign or that trailer. Put your energy where your mouth is and go get the work that you can get! Make the money that is there for you to make and you'll notice that you won't even be thinking about what everyone else is making or doing.

CHAPTER 20

• • •
THE CYCLE OF THE JOB
• • •

> *I did a job for Budget Rent A Car and it was running locally (one market). They paid me for the initial cycle. Then I found out that it was running again. They hadn't paid me. I called my agent, who called the advertising agency, who sent me my cycle fee plus a late charge. You can't always check to make sure that people are honest, but you hope you are getting paid what you should be. (In television, there are people who keep track of when each commercial runs, and who should get paid. In radio, you are more on your own.*

☞ *To get a job, you have to be available for auditions!*

WHO CALLS WHOM?

Casting agents usually call agents the day before the audition. Your agent will then spend a great deal of time, calling voice clients to give them their schedule. A good agent will know your day. My agent always pleasantly surprises me when I go into the office in the morning to read and he says, "So, you've got a 12:00, a 1:15 and a 4:00." He knows my exact day. This is why it is so important to be available. If you cannot be available one hour of one given day, you MUST call your agent and let them know so they can book you out. Otherwise, they will accept an audition for you and you won't show up. The agent looks bad and you look unprofessional.

Communicate with your agent. Emergencies happen, of course, and you can't always get to an audition on time. Call your agent so they can alert the casting. You may be in a group read and are holding up several people. Voice-over actors usually have a busy day running from audition to session—if they're lucky enough to be working and running around—so, they are all on a tight schedule.

Some days, you might not get any calls. That just means there is nothing for you to read. Or, you may just go into your voice agency, read one piece of copy and leave. This is normal. Sometimes it's just slow. Don't panic about it.

Calls can come in any time of the work day. The only time a call won't come in is 9:00 at night or 3:00 in the morning. You usually won't hear from your agent on weekends. The only exception can be promos, which are usually taped in the evening. Writers spend the morning writing the promos, the afternoon getting them approved, and the evening recording them. Promos air very quickly.

Do I Always Have to Audition to Get the Job?

Sometimes, although rarely, you will get a booking from a referral. This usually happens to established voice-over talent whose voice is "out there" a lot. Or, if the person knows you and personally recommends you. More than likely, you will still have to read for the part. You will always be competing for the job with other people.

How Often Should I Bug my Agent?

Don't call your agent all the time. Depending on how much you work and how much you need to talk to your agent—to make or change appointments, to confirm a job—let them do their work! When they are talking to you, they are not talking to casting directors. Call your agent when you need to talk about a specific problem or question. Call your agent once a week to check in. Don't call your agent every day and ask if there is anything for you to come in and read. You have to assume that since they've retained you as a client, they will bring you in when they think you're right for something.

What About Out of Town Jobs?

Your voice-over agent covers all jobs you book, including out of town ones. If you book a job that requires you to fly to Phoenix, Arizona, they will arrange everything.

If you are out of town and somehow book a job there, your agent will still be the one to negotiate and make the commission. It doesn't matter where you go, if you have an agent representing you, that person(s) is still your agent, as long as you are legally bound by contract.

CAN I HAVE DIFFERENT AGENTS IN DIFFERENT CITIES?

It is not unusual for voice-over talent to work in different markets, and you may have different agents representing you in those markets. In that case, the agent who sends you out on the audition would be the one to receive the commission.

If you move, you will need to find another agent to be representing you in that city, but if you are just on vacation and you know of other auditions or your agent sets you up meetings with casting directors in that town, they will still be your agent.

Please note that all of this is up to your agent. If you do not have a signed contract with your agent and you are going back and forth between cities, as long as your agent and you are okay with you being sent out by other people, it's fine. If there is no contract, you are not legally bound.

HOW MUCH WILL I WORK? OR, SHOULD I QUIT MY NIGHT JOB?

Once you are working, your schedule may vary from week to week. You may go to ten auditions one week and none the next. You may be called in to your agency, or around town, every day or two to read. Other days, you may not get. Your agent may not call you one week and the next week you may get several calls. Sometimes there's a lot and sometimes there's not.

Don't be picky about which auditions you'll go to, and which auditions you won't. Let your agent do the picking—he is trying to build a career, just as you are. When you signed together hopefully you talked about your game plan. It was either, "Send me out on everything, I don't care what I book" to "I really want to only do animation." Your agent is now working for you, getting you into the best jobs that are out there, for you to book.

You can definitely go on other auditions, if you come across them. Your agent may not know about a certain audition that a friend tells you about. If your friend sets up the audition, let your agent know, or have your agent call to set up the audition. The agent won't always know about everything that's out there. Keep your ears open! An audition can pass you by. There's nothing you can do about it. Work at meeting all the casting directors you can and getting on their good side, so you don't miss any opportunities.

If you feel as if your agent is only sending you out for radio auditions, talk with him. He may feel that you aren't ready for television copy. Radio is a little easier to break into. It's easier to book with less competition. Once you're reading for television, you are going up against a lot of pros who work a lot. Radio feels a little less intimidating and seems more realistic to newcomers. Don't let this deter you.

ARE THERE SLOW MONTHS?

Because some ad campaigns are done so far in advance and other will be booked and on the air two days later, it's difficult to generalize.

Before the holidays, it gets busy. Haven't you noticed it seems there are more ads running during the holidays? The holidays is one of the biggest shopping seasons. Therefore, you will see more companies trying to push their products with new commercials. More work for you!

WHAT ABOUT VACATIONS?

The best time to take a vacation, if you are going to, is in the late summer months, but try to make them short vacations. You will want to be gone as few weekdays as you can since this is when all the auditions come in. Being gone on long trips keeps you out of competition. Ad agencies won't hold the audition for you until you get into town the following week. Everyone works on a deadline. In short: Be available and hustle! Now, go get them!

• • •
AFTERWORD
• • •

I wrote this book to enlighten people about the voice-over world. I hope I've answered your questions and help you create a fun and lucrative career for yourself in Anytown, USA. I hope I've opened your eyes to some of the "invisible" jobs of voice-overs. No matter where you live, start there. Don't worry about Hollywood, New York or Chicago right off. Focus on getting the bait first. Then worry about the big fish.

GOOD LUCK!

APPENDIX A – SAMPLE COPY

This section includes samples of actual copy for a variety of voice-over work, including TV, radio, promos and more.

Promo Spot #1

E NEWS DAILY 1/30/95	JA	☐ Editor ☒ Anchor 1 ☐ Anchor 2 ☒ Producer
4:46:52 PM	2 0:15 UP NEXT #1 (JB: MARKER)	19

2-SHOT

(PAGE 19) (AMY)

STILL TO COME ON E! NEWS DAILY/ BRAD PITT HOLDS ON TO HIS NUMBER-ONE RANKING./ WE'LL GO PARTYING WITH THE 'MARRIED WITH CHILDREN' CROWD./ THEN: HOW BOYZ-2-MEN SPENT SUPER BOWL SUNDAY./

VO - GRIECO

AND RICHARD GRIECO./ JOINING THE STARSHIIP VOYAGER IN BOLDLY GOING WHERE NO ONE HAS GONE BEFORE./ NEXT./

AT :05, SOUND FULL

(SOT)

OC: "on pcp or something"
TRT: :14 (goes to black)

Chyron: ☒ Completed ☐ Not Needed

BANNER: Coming Up/ Hawaiian Punch

Promo Spot #2

E NEWS DAILY
Mon, May 22, 1995   3:57p

AP	PN **COLD OPEN A**	01

2-SHOT **MUSIC CART THROUGHOUT**	(PAGE 01) FROM LOS ANGELES .. THIS IS E! NEWS DAILY / COMING UP,
TAKE VO **(STARTS ON FREEZE)**	A HUGE OPENING—THE LATEST "DIE HARD" FILM EXPLODES ACROSS THE COUNTRY WITH A VENGEANCE /
SOT @ :05 **OC: "GO NOW PLEASE"** **VO @ :09** /	(SOT) THEN, THE EXPERIMENT AT C-B-S NEWS IS OVER—DAN STAYS, CONNIE LEAVES /
TRT :15	

Chyron: ☐ Completed ☒ Not Needed
/

30-Second TV Spot

8-28-98

Fleet
:30 Tv
Lines of business
"Family feast"

ANNCR: Money can buy you the house on the lake...the car of your dreams, but there are things... you have to build yourself.

Son: (whispering to his dad)
    What do you think about when you look around the table and see us all?

Grandfather: That I'm blessed. Truly blessed.

SUPER: Fleet Investment Group

ANNCR: Private Client Services. Part of Fleet Investment Group. 1800 Call Fleet.

SUPER: Build something.

Older, warm

TV Tag

TEAM ONE ADVERTISING

BROADCAST COPY

CLIENT: LDA
PRODUCT:
JOB NO: LDA-T5-555
DATE: 4/28/95
PAGE 1 OF 1

TITLE: "BOSTON TAG"
MEDIUM: TELEVISION
LENGTH: 10 SECONDS
ACCOUNT REP: MC
REVISION #: 0

(MORPH)

(BOSTON)
See your greater Boston area and New Hampshire dealer today.

60-SECOND RADIO SPOT

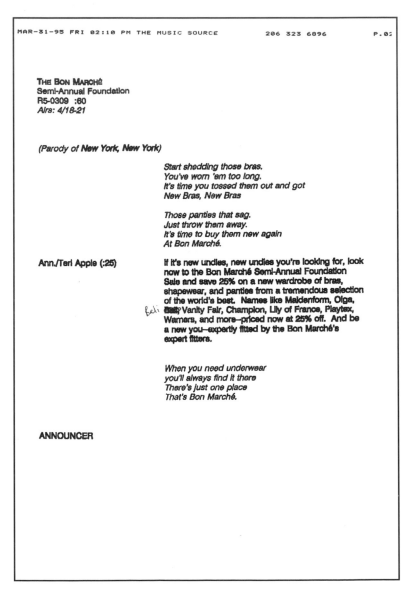

MAR-31-95 FRI 02:10 PM THE MUSIC SOURCE   206 323 6896   P.02

THE BON MARCHÉ
Semi-Annual Foundation
R5-0309 :60
Airs: 4/18-21

(Parody of *New York, New York*)

Start shedding those bras.
You've worn 'em too long.
It's time you tossed them out and got
New Bras, New Bras

Those panties that sag.
Just throw them away.
It's time to buy them new again
At Bon Marché.

Ann./Teri Apple (:25)   If it's new undies, new undies you're looking for, look
now to the Bon Marché Semi-Annual Foundation
Sale and save 25% on a new wardrobe of bras,
shapewear, and panties from a tremendous selection
of the world's best. Names like Maidenform, Olga,
Bali Vanity Fair, Champion, Lily of France, Playtex,
Warners, and more—priced now at 25% off. And be
a new you—expertly fitted by the Bon Marché's
expert fitters.

When you need underwear
you'll always find it there
There's just one place
That's Bon Marché.

ANNOUNCER

30-Second Radio Spot with Celebrity

OCT-27-98 10:55 From: T-458 P.04/07 Job-895

THE MARTIN AGENCY

Copy

Client: YPPA
Job No: 69310019-3
Date: October 23, 1998
Revision No: 1
Job: National Radio
              "Open Letter"
              :30 Radio
Page No: 1

VO: An open letter to America from the author of the Yellow Pages, Mr. Jon Lovitz.

(Heartfelt music)

JON: Dear America. It is with deep humility that I thank you for taking my book to your collective bosom. When I was writing the Yellow Pages, I wanted it to be a place to get ideas. It has succeeded beyond my wildest imaginings....I have seen Greenie the Pet Iguana.

GIRL: Thank you, Mr. Lovitz.

JON: I have seen the sky-diving wedding.

COUPLE: Thank you, Mr. Lovitz.

JON: I have seen...whatever that was I saw in Akron.

MAN: Thank you, Mr. Lovitz.

VO: Get an idea. Open the Yellow Pages.

OPEN LETTER: "GIRL" - 6-8 years old. Clear and unrehearsed.
                          "COUPLE" - Could be the same couple as is Love Story. Young, 20's.
                          "MAN" - Age doesn't matter. A little quirky, but not weird.

VOICEOVER: "VO" - male and female. Matter of fact reads. Confident without being
                          overstated. No age limit. No character.

PLEASE CALL IF YOU HAVE ANY QUESTIONS. THANK YOU VERY MUCH!

60-Second Spanish Radio Spot

JUST READ SPANISH SCRIPT

CLIENT 86484 CELCHI bw   **TITLE** "Clown Feet/Spanish"

MEDIUM Radio   **LENGTH/SIZE:** 60

GSD&M

DATE 11/3/98   **WRITER** RR/HO/JM **PRODUCER**

MUSIC:	**SIMPLE HOLIDAY MUSIC**
KID:	Estaba junto al árbol de Navidad cuando de repente vi los zapatotes de un payaso asomándose en la chimenea.
ANNCR:	Cellular One y Ronald McDonald House Charities de Chicaogoland y Northwest Indiana le tiene una oferta navideña especial.
KID:	Y dije, "Oye, Ronald, entra por la puerta...esa es la entrada privada de Santa Clos."
ANNCR:	Primero, compre un equipo prepagado de Cellular One•2•3 sin verificación de crédito, contratos, ni cuentas mensuales. Luego, al hacer un donativo de $5 a Ronald McDonald House Charities, recibirá gratis 10 minutos de tiempo adicional, y una tarjeta de "raspe-y-gane" con la oportunidad de ganar premios de Cellular One y de los restaurantes McDonald's participantes.
KID:	Entonces, Ronald le explicó a mis papas como podrían ayudar a niños durante la época navideña — y se esfumó. La verdad es que se mueve rápido para un tipo con zapatotes tan grandes.
ANNCR:	Para detalles, llame al 1-800-378-9060 o visite una tienda Cellular One. No se requiere compra para recibir premios. Se aplican términos y condiciones de Cellular One. Oferta por tiempo limitado, hasta agotar existencias.

ANNCR: Male. Adult. Warm, friendly voice with a very natural delivery.

Need 1 (Quantity) audition cassettes delivered by: **Monday 11/9**

CHILDREN'S ANIMATION SPOT

THE HAUNTING OF HILL HOUSE
Soundtrack components 9.21.98
Children's script

Nursery Rhymes

The following rhymes are to read by both a singlar girl's voice and as a chorus of 3 or so children.

"Peter, Peter, pumkin eater
Had a wife and couldn't keep her.
So he put her in a pumpkin shell
And there he kept her very well."

"One, two, buckle my shoe.
Three, four, lock the door.
Five, six, pick up sticks.
Seven, eight, lay them straight.
Nine, ten, home again."

"Ring around the rosie
Pocket full of poseys
Ashes to ashes
We all fall down."

15-Second CD-ROM Spot

<u>**LIONS**</u>

<u>Window</u>

Open on a kid sitting near an open window.
We hear a rustling outside.
A giraffe appears in the window and starts to eat the leaves.
Then a monkey joins him hanging upside down.
Next a lion pops up.
We cut to the outside of the house to see all of the animals
outside the window trying to look in at the boy.

VO:

With Disney's Active Play the *Lion King II: Simba's Pride* CD-ROM...

...everyone will want to play.

MALES, 30-40ISH SOUNDING. FRIENDLY, SWEET, NATURAL -
NOT SALES-LIKE.

APPENDIX B –
FAMOUS NAMES AND VOICES

•••

Billy Zane	Acura
Dick Cavett	AT&T
Tom Selleck	AT&T
Mimi Rogers	AT&T
Howie Mandell	*Bobby's World*
James Earl Jones	The voice of "CNN," Darth Vader
Kathleen Turner	Dr. Pepper, Dove Chocolate
Jason Alexander	*Duckman*
Dweezel Zappa	*Duckman*
Tim Curry	*Duckman*, other animation
James Coburn	Federal Express
Lindsay Wagner	Ford
Jack Lemmon	Honda
Michael Douglas	Infiniti
Demi Moore	Keds, Oscar Meyer
Cybill Shepherd	Mercedes
Roy Scheider	Mercury
Tommy Lee Jones	Red Dog Beer
Sally Kellerman	Seven Seas. Anti Smoking
Robert Stack	Taco Bell
Brenda Vaccaro	Tampax
Julie Kavner	*The Simpsons* (Marge Simpson)
Martin Sheen	Toyota
Gene Hackman	United Airlines
Hector Elizondo	Unocal
Donald Sutherland	Volvo

APPENDIX C – RESOURCES

AGENTS IN LOS ANGELES

Abrams Artists and Associates	(310) 859-1417
Abrams Rubaloff And Lawrence	(213) 935-1700
Cassell-Levy	(213) 461-3971
Commercials Unlimited	(310) 888-8788
Cunningham, Escott, Dipene	(310) 475-2111
International Creative Management	(310) 550-4304
Kazarian Spencer and Assoc/Don Pitts	(818) 755-7569
The William Morris Agency	(310) 859-4124
Sandie Schnarr Talent	(213) 653-9479
Special Artists Agency	(310) 859-9688
Sutton Barth and Vanari	(213) 938-6000
Talent Group	(213) 852-9559
Herb Tannen and Assoc.	(213) 466-6191
Arlene Thorton and Assoc.	(818) 760-6688
Tisherman Agency	(213) 850-6767
The Wallis Agency	(818) 953-4848

UNIONS

AFTRA
National Headquarters
5757 Wilshire Blvd., 9th Floor
Los Angeles, CA 90036
Tel (323) 634-8100

SAG
National Headquarters
5757 Wilshire Blvd.
Los Angeles, CA 90036
Tel (323) 954-1600

Casting Services

Bert Berdis & Company
1956 N. Cahuenga Blvd.
Hollywood, CA 90068
Tel (213) 462-7261

Terry Berland Voice Casting
2050 S. Bundy Ave.
Los Angeles, CA 90025
Tel (310) 571-4141
Fax (310) 820-5408

Carroll Voice Casting
6767 Forest Lawn Drive
Suite 203
Los Angeles, CA 90068
Tel (323) 851-9966
Fax (323) 851-3973

Elaine Craig Voice Casting
6464 Sunset Blvd., Suite1150
Los Angeles, CA 90028
Tel (323) 469-8773
Fax (323) 469-6990

Danny Goldman & Associates Voice Casting
1006 N. Cole Ave.
Los Angeles, CA 90038
Tel (323) 463-1600
Fax (323) 463-3139

Davis/Glick
3280 Cahuenga Blvd. West
2nd Floor
Los Angeles, CA 90068
Tel (213) 851-2233

Marc Graue Voice Casting
3421 W. Burbank Blvd.
Burbank, CA 91505
Tel (818) 953-8991
Fax (818) 953-2805

Kalmenson & Kalmenson Voice-over Casting
5730 Wish Ave.
Encino, CA 91316
Tel (818) 342-6499
Fax (818) 343-1403

Klasky/Csupo
1258 N. Highland Ave.
Hollywood, CA 90038
Tel (213) 463-0145

Bob Lloyd The Voicecaster
1832 W. Burbank Blvd.
Burbank, CA 91506
Tel (818) 841-5300
Fax (818) 841-2085

Sheila Manning Voice Casting
508 S. San Vicente Blvd.
Los Angeles, CA 90048
Tel (323) 852-1046
Fax (323) 852-1013

Dick Orkin's Radio Ranch
1140 N. LaBrea Blvd.
Hollywood, CA 90038
Tel (323) 462-4966

Voices
13261 Moorpark St., Suite 102
Sherman Oaks, CA 91423
Tel (818) 713-9958

*Kris Zimmerman Voice-over
Casting*
1212 N. Cedar St.
Glendale, CA 91207
Tel (818) 956-5505
Fax (818) 956-5507

RECORDING STUDIOS

Alpha Studios
4720 W. Magnolia Blvd.
Burbank, CA 91505
Tel (818) 506-7443

Another Large
5750 Wilshire Blvd., Suite 600
Los Angeles, CA 90036
Tel (213) 954-8500

Audiobanks
1660 9th Street
Santa Monica, CA 90404
Tel (310) 581-1660
Fax (310) 581-1661

Baker Nesbit
451 N. La Cienega Blvd.
Suite 12
Los Angeles, CA 90048
Tel (310) 657-5687

The Bakery
10709 Burbank Blvd.
North Hollywood, CA 91601
Tel (818) 508-7800
Fax (818) 508-7122

Bert Berdis & Company
1956 N. Cahuenga Blvd. West
Hollywood, CA 90068
Tel (213) 462-7261

Bell Sound Studios West
12421 W. Olympic Blvd.
Los Angeles, CA 90064
Tel (310) 826-6333
Fax (310) 826-6004

Buzzy's
6900 Melrose Ave.
Los Angeles, CA 90038
Tel (213) 931-1867

Complete Sound
1438 N. Gower Street
Box 50, Bldg. 48
Hollywood, CA 90028
Tel (323) 860-7600
Fax (323) 860-7698

Davis/Glick
3280 Cahuenga Blvd. West
2nd Floor
Los Angeles, CA 90068
Tel (213) 851-2233

Digital Sound Works
13848 Ventura Blvd. #4-D
Sherman Oaks, CA 91423
Tel (818) 386-9172
Fax (818) 386-9646

Enterprise Studios
4620 W. Magnolia Blvd.
Burbank, CA 91505
Tel (818) 505-6000
Fax (818) 505-6006

Five Guys Named Mo
3500 W. Olive Ave. #1470
Burbank, CA 91505
Tel (818) 955-6637
Fax (818) 955-7067

Four Media Company—4 MC
2901 W. Alameda Ave.
Burbank, CA 91505
Tel (818) 840-7000
Fax (818) 840-7103

Marc Graue Recording
3421 W. Burbank Blvd.
Burbank, CA 91505
Tel (818) 953-8991

Hollywood Digital
6690 Sunset Blvd.
Hollywood, CA 90028
Tel (323) 465-0101
Fax (323) 469-8055

Hollywood Recording Services
6565 Sunset Blvd., 2nd Floor
Hollywood, CA 90028
Tel (323) 957-8400
Fax (323) 957-8410

Dick Orkin's Radio Ranch
1140 N. La Brea Ave.
Los Angeles, CA 90038
Tel (323) 462-4966
Fax (323) 856-4311

Pacific Ocean Post Sound
625 Arizona Ave.
Santa Monica, CA 90401
Tel (310) 458-9192
Fax (310)587-1222

Post Group-West Los Angeles
11858 La Grange Ave.
Los Angeles, CA 90025
Tel (310) 979-4300
Fax (310) 979-4320

SSI/Advanced Post Services
7155 Santa Monica Blvd.
Los Angeles, CA 90046
Tel (323) 874-9344
Fax (323) 850-7189

Voicecaster
1832 W. Burbank Blvd.
Burbank, CA 91506
Tel (818) 841-5300

Voicetrax West
3611 Cahuenga Blvd. West
Los Angeles, CA 90068
Tel (213) 850-1112

Waves
1956 N. Cahuenga Blvd.
Hollywood, CA 90068
Tel (213) 466-6141

Westlake Audio
7265 Santa Monica Blvd.
Los Angeles, CA 90046
Tel (323) 851-9800
Fax (323) 951-9386

World Wide Wadio
6464 Sunset Blvd., Suite 1180
Los Angeles, CA 90028
Tel (323) 957-3399

Training

Adler-Zimmerman Animation Workshop
Burbank, CA
Tel (818) 759-1515

Cindy Akers & Voicetrax West
Cahuenga Pass, CA
Tel (323) 850-1112

Aliso Creek Voice-over Workshop
Burbank, CA
Tel (818) 954-9931

Bob Bergen's Animation Voice-over Workshop
Studio City, CA
Tel (818) 901-8714

Terry Berland's Voice-over Workshops
West Los Angeles
Tel (310) 571-4141

Louise Chamis Voice-over Workshop
Studio City, CA
Tel (818) 985-0130

Dialects & Accents
San Fernando Valley, CA
Tel (818) 772-1746

Robb Holt's Voice-over Workshop
Hollywood, CA
Tel (818) 762-4045

In-Studio Voice-over Workshops
Glendale, CA
Tel (310) 645-9622

Introduction To Voice-overs
Hollywood, CA
Tel (323) 960-3100

Learning Annex
11850 Wilshire Blvd., Suite 100
Los Angeles, CA 90025
Tel (213) 478-6677

Jill Lesly Jones Voice-over Workshop
San Diego, CA
Tel (619) 792-6300

Kat Lehman's Voice-over Workshops
Burbank, CA
Tel (562) 984-8498

Alan K. Lohr's Voice-over Bootcamp
Glendale, CA
Tel (818) 569-5469

Dick Orkin's Practice Practice Workshop
Los Angeles, CA
Tel (323) 462-4966

CASSETTES AND CD DUPLICATION

& Cassette Copies
Tel (818) 508-7578

Abbey Tape Duplicators
9525 Vassar Ave.
Chatsworth, CA 91311
Tel (818) 882-5210

AT & T Duplicating
501 N. Larchmont Blvd.
Los Angeles, CA 90004
Tel (323) 466-9000

Audio Cassette Duplicator Company
12426 1/2 Ventura Blvd.
Studio City, CA 91604
Tel (818) 762-2232

Disc Makers
3445 Cahuenga Blvd. West
Los Angeles, CA 90068
Tel (323) 876-1411

Dynamite Dubs
3611 Cahuenga Blvd. West
Los Angeles, CA 90068
Tel (323) 851-3850

Straight Copy
11390 Ventura Blvd. #6
Studio City, CA 91604
Tel (818) 509-6774

Demo Tape Duplication and J-Card Services

Abbey Tape Duplicators .... (818) 882-5210
AT and T Duplicating .... (213) 466-9000
Audio Cassette Duplicator .... (818) 762-2232
Burbank Print and Copy Center .... (818) 842-5167
Dave And Dave Incorporated .... (818) 508-7578
Dynamite Dubs .... (213) 851-3850
NCI Sound and Video .... (818) 848-1004
Pro WestAudio .... (818) 715-9995
SBQ .... (818) 889-2870
SoundZone .... (818) 558-1144
Straight Copy .... (818) 509-6774
Wilder Brothers .... (310) 557-3500

Loop Groups

Loop Ease, Sandy Holt .... (310) 271-8217
Burt Sharp, Sharp/ADR Services .... (818) 988-3030
Super Loopers, Dee Marcus .... (213) 874-4427

Audio Books

Dove Audio Books .... (213) 487-9953
Books on Tape .... (800) 541-5525

PUBLICATIONS

An excellent resource book for voice-over artists is *The Resource Guide* ($9.99) from Dave Sebastian Williams, an extensive directory of every casting director, agent, production house (promo, animation, trailer, commercial), J-Card services and demo directors, where to make tapes and where to get copies. Send $9.99 to: The Resource Guide, 1770 North Highland Avenue, Suite H648, Hollywood, CA 90028, or call (818) 508-7578.

Advertising Age
Crain Communications
740 Rush Street
Chicago, Il 60617-2590
Tel (888) 298-5900

Animation Magazine
30101 Agoura Court, Suite 110
Agoura Hills, CA 91301-4301
Tel (818) 991-2884

Backstage West/Backstage
1515 Broadway, 14th floor
New York, NY 10036
Tel (212) 764-7300

Broadcasting and Cable Magazine
1705 DeSales Street N.W.
Washington, DC 20036
Tel (202) 659-2340

Electronic Media
Crain Communications
740 Rush Street
Chicago, Il 60617-2590
Tel (888) 298-5900

Fade In:
289 S. Robertson Blvd.
Suite 465
Beverly Hills, CA 90211
Tel (310) 275-0287
Tel (800) 646-3896

Hollywood Reporter
5055 Wilshire Blvd.
Los Angeles, CA 90036-4396
Tel (323) 525-2150

L.A. Actors Line Casting
1515 Broadway, 14th Floor
New York, NY 10036
Tel (212) 764-7300

The Ross Reports
1515 Broadway, 14th Floor
New York, NY 10036
Tel (212) 764-7300

Variety
5700 Wilshire Blvd.
Los Angeles, CA 90036
Tel (323) 857-8600
Fax (323) 965-4476
245 W. 17th Street
New York, NY 10011
Tel (212) 337-7002
Fax (212) 337-7001

• • •

GLOSSARY

• • •

13 week per spot per cycle: You will receive the fee every 13 weeks per spot, per the cycle. So that you are sure to get payment every 13 weeks, you write on contracts, per spot per cycle.

13 weeks: You are paid every 13 weeks that the commercial runs.

15, 30, 60 second reads: Terms for the length of the spot that you are doing. The spots are called reads.

ADR: Audio Dialogue Replacement. Another term for looping or walla.

AFTRA: American Federation Of Radio And Television Artists. Union for actors.

Animatic: The"rough" of the commercial. Not in color, not finished, no music.

Announcer: You are the announcer of the spot.

Authoritative: Make it sound like you know what you're talking about. Keep it informative.

Bleed through: Noise from headphones that are being picked up by the placement of the microphone. Your headphones may be too high or you may be standing in the wrong place and they will make a feed through sound.

Buyout: When you are paid one lump sum for a commercial. No residuals.

Cable: Runs on a cable station only.

Cans: Headphones.

Caress: Play with certain words more. Emphasize longer, elongate, warm the words up.

Cheesy: Will use this term for direction when they want you to push the character out and really go way out.

Class A usage: Top paid. National network usage.

Cone: This is a filter that is Styrofoam and shaped in a cone shape. It goes over the microphone to ensure clear sound.

Conversational: Keep it real. Honest. Phrasing conversationally.

Cut: Stopping a take. More for looping and ADR work.

Cue up: Match to time and speed. At this point, the sound engineer is lining up your voice(s) to the visual and timings of the spot that the ad agency and client want for their spot. They may also be cueing up the music.

DAT: Digital Audio Tape. Clearest kind of tape. Will use a lot for phone patching.

Doublescale: Getting paid double the scale amount.

Doughnut: The insert in a voice-over. Dialogue in the middle between the opening announcer and tag line. You may be hired to do just the "doughnut."

Dubbing: Copying the timing of the foreign film or TV and copying it for the English market.

Feedback: This is a term for the technical sound on a microphone. It would be having feedback or mechanical problems while you're recording. Also, asking you for your opinion, or calling the client for the proper instruction or "Feedback."

Filter: This is what they put on the microphone so that you will sound clearer.

Flat: Type of direction for a read. No emphasis. Monotone.

Full voice: Projecting your entire voice.

Have fun with it: Term that the director will use if they feel you are stiff and need you to relax with the copy.

High energy: They would want you to add energy keep it moving.

Holding fee: You will receive a holding fee check if they want to hold the commercial for possible later air date.

Hot: This term is used when the mike is on. The mike is "Hot."

Intimate: Looking for a softer read. Need to be closer to the microphone.

Landpatch/Phonepatch: This is the digital patching system for a type of read that is all done over the telephone.

Level: The sound engineer will ask for a level, or a sample of how you are going to do the read for the sake of technical.

Local: The local is a chapter that is in that particular state.

Looping: Background sound effects and noises for TV and Film. Done is post production when the show is over.

Mix: Engineer will put the music with the dialogue and edit the entire piece.

Music bed: This is the music that will be laid in the back of the spot.

National: Commercial runs in every state.

National network: Runs in every state on a network station.

Network: Runs on a network affiliate station.

Non-union: Voice-over job that is paid under the table, not through the union. The company did not sign papers. Not a member of SAG or AFTRA.

Off the cuff: Throw the read away. Don't spend so much time on the emphasizing of words. Be more conversational.

On air: Means that you are "Hot" and on with the client for phone patch.

Overscale: Anything that is negotiated that you are paid over the "Scale" amount within the union.

Phones: Just a shorter term for the "headphones."

Pick it up: They want you to hurry up the pace. You're reading a section or the whole thing too slowly.

Placement of the mike: where the microphone will be when you are reading.

Play with: The director may give you this direction to romance or play with a word more.

Playback: Listen back to what has just been recorded.

Pop filter: Just a specific type of filter for Popping of P's attached to the mike to get a clearer read from you.

Promo: The advertising for a TV show, radio program or film.

Pull back: If they feel your pushing the read too much, they will want you to pull back. Keep it simple.

Real: Will want you to keep it conversational and real sounding like real people.

Regional: Spot(s) run in more than one city but not all cities.

Reuse: This is what you are paid for reuse of the spot when they re-run the spot

Rhythm: Looking for the rhythm in the copy.

Romance it: They will use this term when they want you to emphasize a certain word or phrase more.

SAG: Screen Actors Guild. Television union for actors.

Safety: This means that they basically got the read they want, they just want to make sure that they will have very similar reads in case something was technically wrong with the one they love. Once you leave the session and they begin the cutting and editing process, they want to make sure that they have a few choices to work with. It is very common for them to get a "SAFETY" mostly for their own security. Just do the take again, listening to how you did it before. Try to follow the exact same intonation and mood of that read.

Scale: Lowest base union fee for a job.

Scale plus 10: Lowest base union fee plus ten percent commission paid to agent. Will not come out of your base. Extra ten percent from job.

Scratch track: What you watch or listen to that the ad agency has put together for the spot that you are reading to. Not the finished version. May be animatic.

Session fee: Payment for first commercial within the session. If you do two spots, you will receive one session fee and then the payment for the other spot. If you do one spot and two tags, you are paid one session fee and two tag fees. Even if you go to a session just to record two tags, it will be counted automatically as a session plus one tag.

Single: This is a single spot. You are the only one reading the spot.

Slate: What they will get from you in the beginning of the audition. They will have you say your name and agent. Or in a session they will slate the number of the spot each time before you do a take.

Sound booth/sound studio: Recording facility in which you record your voice-over work in.

Sound engineer: The person who works with you in the session for technical and editing. The liaison between talent and client.

Split the difference: A director will tell you this in a session or audition when they are trying to get a read in between of two reads that you already did. They want it somewhere in the middle of the two reads. So they will say "split the difference"

Stand: What you put your copy on in the booth.

Stereotype: When they put you in a certain category or a certain style of read.

Straight read: When they are looking for a business-like, informative read.

Stretch: When they want you to pull the word individually or elongate it.

Sync: Matching your dialogue with another voice or your own voice from an earlier take.

Taft-Hartley: First job with SAG or AFTRA. Protects you from having to join the union until you are hired for two union/AFTRA jobs within 30 days.

Tag: The selling point or highlight phrase of the spot.

Take: This is what they call a reading each time before you read the copy for the session (ex. Take 1, 2, 3, 4, etc.). Also, each recorded version that you do when you're in a session is called a take. The sound engineer will call out, "Take #1, 2, 3" and so on, before each time you begin the spot.

Three in a row: You may need to re-do a word or a phrase in the session or audition. They will have you do Three in a row. A B and C

Time code: A digital time code that can be seen on the sound engineers board. Helps the actors with timings while reading dialogue.

Timing: The timing that you get the spot read in. They say this is a 37 second read. You need to get the spot in that time.

Tone: The sound that you are through the read.

Tracks: Any type of music, background noise, laugh-tracks, that the sound engineer has to use for edits on spots.

Trailer: What you hear in a theater promoting a film.

Union: Organization for actors. Belonging to and working within organizations rules.

Voice matching: Matching the actors voice. (See also Dubbing and Looping)

Wildline: Specific lines recorded at that time within an entire commercial.

Wildspot: A flat fee for a spot that runs an unspecified number of times in a thirteen week cycle. Can be local, regional or national.

OTHER FILM & ENTERTAINMENT BOOKS
FROM IFILM PUBLISHING . . .

◼ ACTING ◼

NEXT!
An Actor's Guide to Auditioning
by Ellie Kanner and Paul G. Bens, Jr.

Written by two of Hollywood's hottest casting directors, NEXT! is the definitive insider's guide to successfully navigating the complicated maze of auditions and landing that all-important role in a movie or TV show. NEXT! details the common errors that most inexperienced actors make when auditioning.

ELLIE KANNER cast the TV pilot of *Friends* and *The Drew Carey Show*.
PAUL G. BENS, JR. is a partner in Melton/Bens Casting.

$19.95 ISBN 0-943728-71-1, original trade paper, 7 x 9, 184 pp.

YOUR KID OUGHT TO BE IN PICTURES
A How-To Guide for Would-Be Child Actors and Their Parents
by Kelly Ford Kidwell and Ruth Devorin

Written by a top talent agent and a stage mom with three children working in film, TV and commercials, YOUR KID OUGHT TO BE IN PICTURES explains what the odds of success are, how to secure an agent, where to go for professional photographs, the auditioning process, lots of photographs, plus much more.

$16.95 ISBN 0-943728-90-8, original trade paper, 9 x 6, 280 pp.

◼ DIRECTING ◼

A CUT ABOVE: 50 FILM DIRECTORS
TALK ABOUT THEIR CRAFT
by Michael Singer; Foreword by Leonard Maltin

Michael Singer takes the reader on an inside look at the craft, art, passion and vision of 50 great film directors. Candid, unrestrained converations weave a personal, never-before-seen intimacy to each interview. This collection of elite artists from Hollywood and around the world elucidates significant developments in filmmaking and sheds a surprising new light on many familiar faces.

MICHAEL SINGER is an entertainment freelance journalist who has written many Making Of... books based upon studio film releases.

$19.95 ISBN 1-58065-000-7, original trade paper, 6 x 9, 224 pp.

**To order or for more information,
call 800.815.0503 or go to www.ifilmpro.com**

OTHER FILM & ENTERTAINMENT BOOKS
FROM IFILM PUBLISHING . . .

▮▮▮ SCREENWRITING ▮▮▮

ELEMENTS OF STYLE FOR SCREENWRITERS
The Essential Manual for Writers of Screenplays
by Paul Argentini

In the grand tradition of Strunk and White's *Elements of Style,* Paul Argentini presents an essential reference masterpiece in the art of clear and concise principles of screenplay formatting, structure and style for screenwriters. Argentini explains how to design and format manuscripts to impress any film school professor, story editor, agent, producer or studio executive. The ultimate quick reference guide to formatting a screenplay.

PAUL ARGENTINI is a screenwriter, playwright and novelist.

$11.95 ISBN 1-58065-003-1, original trade paper, 5.5 x 8.5, 176 pp.

SECRETS OF SCREENPLAY STRUCTURE
by Linda J. Cowgill

In her new book, Linda Cowgill articulates the concepts of successful screenplay structure in a clear language, based on the study of great films from the thirties to present day. SECRETS OF SCREENPLAY STRUCTURE helps writers understand how and why great films work as well as how great form and function can combine to bring a story alive. Cowgill includes many helpful anecdotes, insider strategies, do's and don'ts, all of which will help readers make their writing more professional, and therefore, more marketable.

LINDA J. COWGILL is the author of *Writing Short Films*. She received her Masters in Screenwriting from UCLA after winning several screenwriting awards and fellowships.

$16.95 ISBN 1-58065-004-X, original trade paper, 6 x 9, 336 pp.

GET PUBLISHED! GET PRODUCED!
Tips on how to sell your writing
from America's #1 Literary Agent
by Peter Miller

This valuable book tells how to avoid being viewed as a neophyte in a business notorious for taking advantage of writers. Drawing on over 20 years' experience as a top literary agent, Miller offers advice on how to sell your published fiction, structure a nonfiction book proposal, package your book to become a feature film or TV production, market a screenplay, get an agent, tips on contract negotiation, and more!

PETER MILLER has sold over 800 books on behalf of many best-selling authors, sold book rights for film and TV adaptation and produced several film and TV projects.

$19.95 ISBN 0-943728-92-4, original trade paper, 6 x 9, 336 pp.

**To order or for more information,
call 800.815.0503 or go to www.ifilmpro.com**

OTHER FILM & ENTERTAINMENT BOOKS
FROM IFILM PUBLISHING . . .

▮ SCREENWRITING ▮

WRITING GREAT CHARACTERS
The Psychology of Character Development
by Michael Halperin, Ph.D.

This valuable book will help writers create characters so real
they truly jump off the page. Halperin has developed an easy
to understand system which gives all screenwriters a foolproof,
failproof method of developing great characters. WRITING
GREAT CHARACTERS is a book for all writers, from the expert
who is looking to polish his techniques to the novice who
wants to learn the craft from an expert.

MICHAEL J. HALPERIN, Ph.D., has taught screenwriting at UCLA and
currently teaches at Loyola Marymount University in Los Angeles, CA. He has written numerous
TV programs and authored several bestselling interactive media programs. He holds a BA in
Communications from USC and a Ph.D. in Film Studies from the Union Institute in Cincinnati, OH.

$19.95 ISBN 0-943728-79-7, original trade paper, 6 x 9, 208 pp.

WRITING SHORT FILMS
Structure and Content for Screenwriters
by Linda J. Cowgill

Contrasting and comparing the differences and similarities
between feature films and short films, WRITING SHORT FILMS
offers readers the essential requirements necessary to make
their writing crisp, sharp and compelling. Emphasizing characters, structure, dialogue and story, WRITING SHORT FILMS
dispels the "magic formula" concept that screenplays can be
constructed by anyone with a word processor and a script
formatting program. Writing a good screenplay, short or
long, is a difficult job. With examples from short films and feature films,
the author teaches strategies to keep a short film on track and writer's block at bay.

LINDA J. COWGILL holds a Masters in Screenwriting from UCLA. She has taught screenwriting
seminars at the Boston Film Institute, the American Film Institute, and the prestigious Kennedy
Center in Washington, D.C., and currently teaches screenwriting at Loyola Marymount
University in Los Angeles.

$19.95 ISBN 0-943728-80-0, original trade paper, 6 x 9, approx. 250 pp.

HOW TO ENTER SCREENPLAY CONTESTS. . . AND WIN!
An Insider's Guide to Selling Your Screenplay to Hollywood
by Erik Joseph

There are more than 50 legitimate screenwriting competitions
across the U.S. Entering such a contest is the best and most
affordable way to get your screenplay noticed, optioned, sold,
and ultimately produced. Contains comprehensive listings of
screenplay contests.

$16.95 ISBN 0-943728-88-6, original trade paper, 6 x 9, 184 pp.

**To order or for more information,
call 800.815.0503 or go to www.ifilmpro.com**

OTHER FILM & ENTERTAINMENT BOOKS
FROM IFILM PUBLISHING . . .

▮ PRODUCTION ▮

FILM PRODUCTION:
THE COMPLETE *UNCENSORED* GUIDE TO INDEPENDENT FILMMAKING
by Greg Merritt

Too much of what passes for movie-making instruction is either an empty pep talk or a collection of impractical generalities. This book cuts through the fluff and provides the reader with real-world facts about producing and selling a low-budget motion picture ($500,000 and under). The book covers the complete management of a production from pre-production to principal photography to post-production through distribution. Includes chapters on Raising Money, Scheduling and Budgeting, Publicity and Festivals, Cast and Crew, Trouble Shooting and more.

$24.95 ISBN 0-943728-99-1, original trade paper, 6 x 9, 240 pp.

BREAKING & ENTERING
Land Your First Job in Film Production
by April Fitzsimmons, Foreword by Gale Anne Hurd

An insider's guide to learning the ropes and gaining the proper tools and information to successfully enter into the fiercely competitive business of film production. This book is a great "A to Z" introduction for anyone who wants to get their feet wet in the entertainment industry. Full of hands-on information that pertains to day-to-day operations on the set during film or TV production . . . Real stuff, presented in a cool manner from an experienced pro.

$17.95 ISBN 0-943728-91-6, original trade paper, 6 x 9, 224 pp.

NEW EDITION...
THE FILM EDITING ROOM HANDBOOK, 3rd Ed.
How to Manage the Near Chaos of the Cutting Room
by Norman Hollyn

Editing is the creative force of filmic reality. Veteran Hollywood film editor Norman Hollyn has updated his well-written, semi-technical and profusely illustrated book. One of the most popular books used by film school instructors. The new chapters detail the procedural, creative and technical fundamentals of editing moving images within a computer-based, interactive environment, including an explanation of what nonlinear editing is, how it works, the creative flexibility it offers, and the time and cost savings it can achieve.

$24.95 ISBN 1-58065-006-6, original trade paper, 6 x 9, 448 pp, illustrated, bibliography, index.

• • •
ABOUT THE AUTHOR
• • •

Terri Apple is one of the top voice-over actresses in the country. Her HomeBase campaign created a whole new sound in voice-overs and for advertisers everywhere. Her "Don't even think about it, baldy," commercial for The California Milk Advisory won an Obie award and her work is heard every day all across the country. She has had as many as twenty commercials running simultaneously across the nation, as well as doing promos for CBS, ABC and more. She has been doing voice-overs for over fifteen years and started in the voice-over field while living in Kansas City. She wrote this book to show no matter where you live, there is work. You just have to know how to find it.

Some of her voice-overs include: HomeBase, Milk, Del Monte, Toyota, Mazda, Pontiac, Surf Detergent, Kraft, Michelob, National Rental Car, Budget Rent A Car, Nationwide Insurance, Blue Cross, Archway Cookies, Kellogg's, Venture, JC Penney, Cornnuts, McCormick Spices, California Avocado, Rosetta Pasta, Rosarita Refried Beans, Airwalk, Lifetime, Gabrielle, Friskies Cat Food, and many more.